CAPPER

CLASSICS

A Capper Classic

Capper Classics is a series preserving popular books from the past in quality reprint editions for the modern reader.

This *Capper Classic* edition of *Capper's Farmer Country Cook Book* is a reprint of the revised 1928 edition. The text of the original book is reprinted here unchanged; we have added a new cover and preface, an index, have slightly altered the title page, and have increased the size of the book for easier reading.

Printed on acid-free paper, this *Capper Classic* will make a permanent addition to your home library.

Capper's Farmer Country Cook Book

A REPRINT OF THE REVISED 1928 EDITION

Every recipe in this book is a tried and
tested recipe from some Capper's Farmer
housewife.

CAPPER PRESS
Topeka, Kansas

Copyright © 1928 by Capper Publications

Cover and Text Art by Juline

Cover Design by Diana Edwardson and Kathy Snyman
Copyright © 1989 by Capper Press

Published by
Capper Press, 616 Jefferson, Topeka, Kansas 66607

ISBN 0-941678-20-2

Printed and bound in the United States of America

For information on Capper Press titles, or to place an order, please call
(Toll-Free) 1-800-777-7171, extension 107, or (913) 295-1107

Preface

This cookbook was originally published by *Capper's Farmer* magazine, which was a sister publication of *Capper's Weekly* magazine and which served the farm communities of America for sixty-eight years before closing its doors in 1957.

We are reprinting the popular *Capper's Farmer Country Cook Book* (the 1928 revised edition) because we want to preserve this glimpse into America's fast-vanishing rural way of life. Modern interest in this book was brought to our attention by the readers of *Capper's* magazine (formerly *Capper's Weekly*), many of whom wrote to us over the last several years asking where they might find copies of this classic, one of their favorite old cookbooks. Like those readers (who happen to be terrific cooks), we also feel that modern cooks and cookbook collectors will enjoy this taste from farm kitchens past.

With over 430 recipes, this farm kitchen classic presents wonderful ways to prepare all the vegetables, fruits, and meats that were commonly produced on the farm, plus recipes for canning the way grandma did, and farm-tested household hints and remedies.

A delight for the cookbook collector, *Capper's Farmer Country Cook Book* does, however, present a challenge or two for the adventurous modern cook. Although these recipes were used, as the original preface proclaimed, "by farm women around the country" and "have been tried and tested in actual kitchens and so they are known to be good and practicable," early recipes are not as specific as modern recipes regarding measurements, pan size, oven temperatures, and instructions. So, keeping those words of caution in mind, use good cooking sense when preparing these recipes, and you will have great fun in your kitchen, but even more fun at your table.

Tammy Dodson
CAPPER PRESS
1989

CONTENTS

Abbreviations Used in Recipes in Capper's Farmer Country Cook Book

tsp.—teaspoonful
tbsp.—tablespoonful
c.—cup

lb.—pound
pt.—pint
qt.—quart

All measurements in this book are level.

2 c. equals 1 pt.
1 tbsp. sugar equals 1 oz. flour

4 c. equals 1 lb.
2 c. granulated sugar equals 1 lb.
2 c. butter equals 1 lb.

Capper's Farmer
Country Cook Book

—: :—

BEVERAGE

Pineapple Mint Sauce

1 c. crushed pineapple   ¾ c. water
1 c. sugar   6 drops oil of peppermint

Drain pineapple and put through food chopper unless it is in very small pieces. Pack in a cup, adding enough of the syrup to fill the cup. Put the sugar with it in a sauce pan and color a brilliant green. Add water and simmer 10 min and cool and add oil of peppermint and chill. This makes almost 1 pt. and it may be kept for some time in a cool place. Serve on ice cream or use to flavor ginger ale or lemonade.—Etta Lea Spratt, Texas.

Vienna Chocolate

Put in coffee pot and set in boiling water, 1 qt. new milk (or 1 pt.. each of cream and milk). Stir into it 3 heaping tbsp. Baker's chocolate mixed to a paste with cold milk. Let it boil 2 or 3 min. and serve at once. To make good chocolate good material is required.—Mrs. A. H. Shepard, N. Dak.

California Fruit Cup

Equal quantities of orange, grape fruit, pineapple, banana and white cherries, cut in small pieces. Cover with grape juice and serve very cold. If perfectly ripe no sugar is required. May be added if desired.—Mrs. P. E. Lewis, Calif.

Strawberry Syrup
(For cold drinks, ices, etc.)

2 qts. ripe strawberries   2 lbs. sugar (4 c.)
1 c. water

Put sugar and water on to boil. Boil slowly until it spins a thread. Remove scum while boiling. Mash the berries thru a strainer and add juice to the syrup. Bring to the boiling point quickly. Skim. Boil 5 min. Put into sterilized bottles and when cool, seal with paraffin.—Mrs T. V. Hays, Texas.

Hot Weather Punch

This is simple to make, inexpensive and delicious. To 1 qt. of water add ¾ c. of sugar and the juice of 3 lemons, and 3 oranges, 1 c. grape juice or other fruit juice. Chill before serving.—Mrs. R. A. Fransher, Okla.

Breakfast Coffee (not strong)

Use an absolutely clean coffee pot and allow 1 rounded tbsp. coffee to 1 c. boiling water. Be sure the water is boiling, and after it has been poured over the coffee allow the pot to stand on the stove where it will keep hot, without boiling, for 10 min. Then serve with boiling hot milk and sugar. Coffee made this way will be clear, have a fragrant aroma and delicious flavor.—Mrs. A. L. Dawkins, Mo.

Iced Cocoa for Thirty

3 c. boiling water   ¾ c. cocoa
2½ c. sugar

Stir till well dissolved, place in double boiler and cook 30 min. Cool and add 1 tbsp. vanilla and 6 qt. scalded milk. Chill, beat well. Serve in chilled glasses, place a spoonful cracked ice in each glass, add cocoa and top with whipped cream.—Miss Carrie Wenning, N. Dak.

Cocoa

1½ tbsp. cocoa   1 tbsp. cornstarch
¼ c. sugar   1 c. water
Pinch salt   3 c. milk

Scald milk in a double boiler. Mix the remaining ingredients in a sauce pan and boil for 5 min. Then add to the scalded milk and steam in a double boiler 15 min. Serve hot. Beat thoroly with a dover egg beater before serving. Whipped cream or marshmallows add to its appearance.—Mrs. Chas. Oakes, N. Dak.

Boiled Coffee

½ c. ground coffee   White and shell of 1 egg
½ c. cold water   6 c. boiling water

Scald coffee pot. Put in coffee, egg, shell and ½ of cold water. Mix well, add boiling water and boil 3 to 5 min. Add remainder of cold water and set in a warm place 10 min.—Mrs. Chas. H. Oakes, N. Dak.

Orangeade

2 oranges   ½ c. sugar
1 lemon   ½ c. water
2 c. ice water

Out of ½ c. water and the sugar make a syrup by boiling together 3 min. Add the strained fruit juice and the cold water and chill thoroly. Add any kind of fruit juice to improve the taste and appearance.—Mrs. Chas. Oakes, N. Dak.

Root Beer

Dissolve 3 to 5 cakes of yeast foam and 3 tbsp. sugar in 1 pt. of lukewarm water. Keep in a warm place 12 hr. Stir well. Strain thru cheese cloth. Rinse yeast left on cloth several times with water and throw away solid particles. To dissolve yeast rinsing water add bottle of root beer extract. 4 lbs. of sugar, 5 gal. of lukewarm water. Mix thoroly and bottle at once. Keep in a warm place for 48 to 72 hr. Cool for use and keep in cold place.—Miss Eva Galdale, S. Dak.

Roman Punch for 50

4 doz. lemons
(juice and pulp)
1 doz. oranges
(juice and pulp)
10 lbs. sugar

1 lb. white grapes seeded
2 qt. grape juice
2 qt. canned cherries
4 cans grated pineapple

Place all in a large stone jar. When ready to serve add 4 gal. water and several slices oranges and lemons and ice.—Mrs. Geo. Wiggins, Kansas.

Blackberry Nectar

Take 12 lb. of berries and thoroly crush. Pour over this 1 qt. boiling water and let stand 12 hr. or over night. Next morning strain thru a muslin bag, let drip thoroly but do not squeeze. To each measure of this liquid or juice, add the same amount of sugar and to the entire contents add 5 oz. of tartaric acid. Bottle and seal. When ready to serve. Add 2 tbsp. of this liquid to a glass of crushed ice and water and sweeten to taste. —Mrs. T. V. Hays, Texas.

Mint Raspberry Punch

¼ c. orange juice
½ c. lemon
½ c. sugar

1 tbsp. raspberry flavor
½ doz. sprigs fresh mint
1 pt. cold water

Mix fruit juices well with sugar, and raspberry flavoring. Stir and add water. Pour over large pieces of ice, serve with a sprig of mint in each glass.—Ruth A. Austin, Wis.

Grape Fruit and Cherry Cup

Dice grape fruit and sweeten and add chopped candied cherries. Place in cup with whole cherries (marachino) in center of top and chill before serving.—Mrs. Z. W. Tindle, Ore.

BREAD

This is a tried and true bread recipe and as I have used it many years will send it in, hoping others will have as good luck with it as I do. For a medium sized loaf it will require:

1 c. liquid
3 c. flour
¼ cake dry yeast
1 tbsp. sugar
1 tbsp. shortening
1 tsp. salt

Soak the yeast cake in ½ c. warm water until it is soft and crumbly. Put it in a bread bowl or mixer, add 1½ c. warm liquid (not hot) and 3 c. flour. Beat together until it is smooth and glossy, cover and set sponge in warm place over night. In the morning, mix sugar, salt and shortening with one c. of liquid for every loaf (counting the liquid used in sponge). Stir all together good and add to sponge, then add the necessary amount of flour, mixing thoroughly until you have a soft but firm mass, turn out onto a lightly floured bread board and knead lightly but firmly. Cover and set in a warm place and let rise to double in bulk. Knead it down and let rise again. When light, knead into loaves, let rise until light and bake 1 hr.—Mrs. Tillye C. Burchard, Illinois.

Ice Box Rolls

2 eggs
½ c. sugar
1 c. mashed potatoes
1 c. sweet milk
1 cake compressed yeast
½ c. shortening
2 tsp. salt

Beat the eggs separately and very light. Make sponge, using all ingredients except egg whites, add them last, flour enough for sponge. Let rise and then add enough flour to make dough not quite as stiff as for bread. Let rise. Then put on bread board and roll out and cut like biscuits. Spread with grease and a little sugar and cinnamon if desired. If these are to be kept several days add ½ tsp. soda, and 1 tsp. baking powder and cover tightly. Put in ice box to keep.—Lily B. Dorman, Colorado.

Whole Wheat Bread

2 cakes compressed yeast
¼ c. luke warm water
1 qt. sweet milk
⅓ c. brown sugar
2 tbsp. salt
6 tbsp. butter

3 c. flour, white
5½ c. whole wheat flour, fine, or
(4 c. white flour)
(4 or 5 c. coarse whole wheat flour)

Scald milk in double boiler with sugar, butter and salt. Cool to luke warm. Soak yeast in water and add to milk in bowl. Add enough whole wheat flour to make a batter. Beat thoroughly; add rest of whole wheat and white flour, to knead. The dough should be of a softer consistency than light bread dough. Do not leave actually sticky, however. Knead for 10-15 min., put in greased bowl, cover and let rise at a temperature of 80-85 degrees, till double in bulk. Knead down slightly without adding more flour, cover and let rise again until double in size. Make into loaves and put in well greased individual bread pans. Brush tops with any cooking fat. Cover and let rise till double in bulk. Bake 45 min. in moderate oven, (375 degrees).—Mrs. Julia Diederick, Colorado.

Raisin Bread

3 cakes compressed yeast
2 qt. liquid, ½ water and ½ milk
1½ c. sugar
⅔ c. lard or other shortening
2 tbsp. salt

1 tsp. grated nutmeg
3 eggs
1 lb. seeded or seedless raisins
⅓ c. shredded candied citron, orange or lemon

Some nuts also if desired

Soak yeast in some warm water just enough to cover it in a cup. Scald milk and while still warm add shortening, 1 tbsp. salt and sugar, then the water. Have mixture luke warm, then thicken with flour as other sponges, beat well and mix in the yeast. Cover and set in warm place until light which will be about 45 min. Add beaten eggs to mixture and about 1 qt. of warm water or milk. Sift in flour containing sugar, salt, and nutmeg, beating with a spoon until stiff. Then stir in raisins, making sure they have been perfectly cleaned, and candied citron. Again set in warm place. When light about twice its bulk put in well greased pans round ones are the best 1½ qt. size pudding pans. Let stand in a warm place ½ hr. and bake as other bread 1 hr. for a moderate sized loaf. Do not be afraid of using too much yeast. It is best to buy it from the bakery ¼ lb at a time as it may be kept in the refrigerator and is always handy for quick rolls, etc. We save the water potatoes are boiled in and use in the above recipe. A slice of the above plain or toasted with a glass of milk is a well balanced meal.— Miss Hattie M. Thomas, Texas.

German Apple Cake

4 apples (pared and cut in quarters)
To 4 c. bread dough add

½ c. butter   2 eggs
¼ c. sugar   ¼ c. flour

Roll dough ¾ thickness. Place in shallow pan. Press sharp edge of apples into the dough. Sprinkle with sugar, let rise until dough is double bulk. Place in shallow pan and bake 30 min. in a moderate oven.—Mrs. K. Baxter, Washington.

Butterscotch Rolls

1 cake compressed yeast   1 tsp. salt
1 c. milk scalded and   2 c. flour
    cooled

Mix and let rise about 2 hrs. Cream ¼ c. sugar and ¼ c. butter, add to sponge with 2 eggs well beaten and enough flour to stiffen. Let rise 2 hrs. Mix down, when risen to double its bulk roll out ¼ inch thick and spread with butter and sprinkle generously with brown sugar. Roll like jelly roll and cut in 1 inch slices. Place cut side down in well buttered pan and let rise until light. Bake in rather quick oven.—Mrs. Leo J. Hoffman, Illinois.

Potato Yeast

6 potatoes   1 c. sugar
1 qt. flour   2 tbsp. salt
3 qt. boiling water   3 cakes dry yeast

Dissolve dry yeast in lukewarm water. Pour boiling water over the flour. Stir vigorously, when lukewarm add the boiled potatoes which have been rubbed through a sieve or a potato ricer, sugar, salt and yeast. Use 1 c. yeast to 1 qt. liquid. This is best kept 2 days before using. If kept air-tight in a cool place will keep good for 3 or 4 weeks.—Mrs. Arthur Oettinger, Wisconsin.

Buttermilk Yeast

2 cakes dry yeast soaked in lukewarm water
2 c. buttermilk
2 c. yellow corn meal (white cornmeal may be used, as well)

Let buttermilk come to a boil and stir in the corn meal. Let simmer 10 min. and remove from fire and cool. Add yeast. Roll on board and cut in small pieces and let dry. Do not freeze, before dry. Use same as yeast foam.—Mae Collett, North Dakota.

Salt Rising Bread

At night take ½ c. cornmeal, pinch salt and soda. Scald with new milk heated to the boiling point and mix to thickness of mush. Set in warm place over night. In morning take 1 gal. jar, in this put

1 c sweet milk	1 tsp. sugar
1 tsp. salt	Scald with
3 c water heated to boiling point	

Use a milk thermometer and reduce the temperature to 108 degrees with cold water. Add flour to make a good batter. Now mix in the starter made the night before. Cover with plate. Place the jar in a large kettle of warm water and keep this water at a temperature of 108 degrees) until the sponge rises. It should rise about 2 in. then mix to a stiff dough. Make into loaves, grease well and put into pans. Be careful not to let the heat get out of the loaves while working. Set in warm place to rise, then bake in medium oven 1 hr. and 10 min. Success is sure if this batter and dough is kept at the right temperature until ready to bake.—Mrs. Carrie Cooper, Kansas.

Quick Kneadless Bread

2 cakes compressed yeast	⅓ c. sugar
2 c. milk (lukewarm)	1 tsp. salt
2 qt. flour	1 tbsp. lard

Break yeast into 1 c. lukewarm milk and add 1 tbsp. sugar. Let stand 15 min. Sift flour into mixing bowl. Make a hollow in the center into which place lard and salt, the remainder of sugar and milk. The milk should be warm, add yeast, mix gradually until it can be handled. Leave covered 15 min. Butter a large bowl, turn the dough in to it and butter top of dough. Allow it to rise double the size. Make into loaves and place in buttered pans. Let rise again and bake in hot oven for ¾ hr. Use this same recipe for raisin and prune bread. But use coffee instead of milk, putting in ½ tsp. cinnamon and ½ tsp. allspice. Work in well beaten egg and butter size of egg. Work in cup of raisins and ½ c. stewed prunes. Let rise 1 hr., then bake ¾ hr. in moderate oven.—Mrs. Leota Koch, Kansas.

CAKE

There are several factors in making cakes successfully. First of all the measurements must be accurate. Unless care is taken in measuring the various ingredients which, when combined, make a cake, the cake is apt to not be a success.

The shortening used in the cake may be butter, lard, oleomargerine, or any vegetable shortening. If any of the butter substitutes are used, additional salt should be added to the recipe. Milk is generally the liquid used, although water, coffee, or fruit juices may be used. Cake made with pastry flour is usually lighter and smoother in texture, than cake made with bread flour. Pastry flour is made from spring wheat and contains more starch. Better pastries and cakes both, are made from flour which contains more of the starch than gluten.

Layer cakes should bake 15 to 30 minutes, according to the thickness of the layer.

Loaf cakes should bake ¾ to 1½ hours.

Cold Water White Cake

2 c. sugar
½ c. butter
1 c. water

2½ c. flour
2 tsp. baking powder
4 eggs

1 tsp. extract

Cream butter and sugar, add water alternately with flour and baking powder, which has been sifted together. Add extract and lastly fold in stiffly beaten egg whites. Bake in moderate oven (375°).—Mrs. August W. Ehrens, N. Dak.

Marble Angel Food Cake

1¼ c. egg white
1 c. and 2 tbsp. sugar
½ tsp. salt
1 tsp. cream tartar
½ c. flour
½ tsp. vanilla

Yellow Part
6 egg yolks
⅔ c. flour
½ tsp. orange juice

Sift flour once, measure, sift 4 times, put egg whites on platter, beat until foamy, add salt and cream tartar. Beat stiff but not dry, carefully fold in sugar. Divide whites into 2 parts. To 1 part fold in ½ c. flour and ½ tsp. vanilla. To other part fold in 6 beaten egg yolks, ⅔ c. flour and ½ tsp.

orange juice (or extract). Put by spoonful in marble style, in ungreased angel food pan. Bake 50 to 60 min. in slow oven (300°). Invert pan, allow to cool 1 hr. before removing.—Mrs. J. N. Scrivner, Texas.

Lady Baltimore

3 c. flour	½ c. milk
3 tsp. baking powder	½ c. water
¼ tsp. salt	1 tsp. vanilla
½ c. butter	¼ tsp. almond
1⅔ c. sugar	3 egg whites

Sift flour once before measuring, add baking powder and salt, sift three times. Cream butter and sugar, gradually add milk, water and flour alternately. Add flavoring, fold whites of eggs in carefully. Bake in moderate oven (375°) in three layers. Icing: ¼ lb. figs, ½ lb. raisins, ½ lb. walnut meats, 2 c. sugar, ¾ c. water, 2 egg whites, 1 tsp. vanilla. Boil sugar and water until forms a hard ball in water pour over egg whites beat until creamy, add raisins, figs, walnut meats and vanilla while beating.—Miss Pauline Frazier, Mo.

Mahogany Cake

Dissolve:	4 eggs
2 oz. chocolate in	½ c. sweet milk
5 tbsp. boiling water	1¾ c. flour
½ c. butter	2 tsp. baking powder
1½ c. sugar	

Cream butter with sugar, add to this the well beaten egg yolk, and cooked chocolate mixture. Sift flour with baking powder, and alternately add with the milk to the above mixture. Lastly fold in egg whites. Bake in moderate oven (375°). Filling: Cream 3 c. powdered sugar with ½ c. butter, yolk of 1 egg, 2 tbsp. powdered chocolate mixed with 5 tbsp. strong hot coffee, stir well; add 2 tsp. vanilla and 2 tsp. sweet cream. Beat until smooth and light. Just before putting the cake into cook, stir your finger gently in each layer, 3 times.—Mrs. Earl Rutherford, Texas.

Fudge Cake

2 squares of grated chocolate or ½ c. cocoa. Add ½ c. boiling water and tsp. soda. When chocolate is dissolved, add 2 c. brown sugar and ½ c. butter and 3 eggs (putting in 1 at a time), and beating thoroughly.

½ c. sour milk	1 tsp. cinnamon
1 tsp. vanilla	1⅓ tsp. nutmeg
2 c. flour (sifted 5 times)	¼ tsp. cloves

Mix all together and beat thoroly. Bake in moderately hot oven (375°). I omit the spices and use cocoa and have a rich, dark cake.—Mrs. Ben Krouse, Wis.

Southern Date Cake

½ c. evaporated milk
½ c. water
2 tsp. baking powder
3 c. flour
1½ c. sugar
5 eggs beaten separately
1 c. butter
1 tsp. vanilla

Cream the butter until very light and add the sugar and cream mixture. Add the well beaten egg yolks. Dilute the milk with water and add alternately with flour mixed and sifted with the baking powder, then the vanilla and fold in the well beaten egg whites. Bake in 3 layers. Filling: ½ c. evaporated milk, ½ c. water, 2 c. brown sugar, 1 tsp. vanilla, 1 c. English walnuts (chopped fine), ¼ c. butter, 1 c. stoned dates. Dilute the milk with the water, add the sugar and butter and cook until it makes a soft ball in water. Remove at once from fire and add dates, and nuts and beat. Add vanilla and beat until cool, then pour on layers.—Mrs. C. J. Lowe, Ohio.

Red Devil's Food Cake

¼ c. shortening
1 c. sugar
½ c. sour milk
½ c. cocoa
½ c. boiling water
2 well beaten egg yolks
Mix cocoa with boiling water
1½ c. flour
1 tsp. soda
1½ tsp. baking powder
1 tbsp corn starch

Cream shortening and sugar, add egg yolks well beaten. Then add cocoa mixture. Sift soda, baking powder and cornstarch with flour. Beat hard then fold in whites. Makes nice layer cake or can be baked in loaf.—Mrs. W. J. Wiley, Iowa.

Date Cake

½ c. dates
½ c. raisins
1 c. hot water
Cook until quite thick
3 eggs
1 c. sugar
½ c. lard
1 tsp. soda
2 tsp. baking powder
2 c. flour

Let cooked mixture cool. Beat eggs, sugar, and lard. Sift soda and baking powder with flour. Add this to egg mixture and then add the cooked mixture to this. Bake in layer cake pans in moderate oven.—Helen Kessler, Wis.

Eggless Dark Cake

2 c. brown sugar
½ c. butter or lard
½ c. cocoa
½ c. hot water
1 c. sour milk or
buttermilk
1 tsp. soda (dissolved in 1 tbsp. cold water)
1 tsp. vanilla
2½ c. flour

Cream butter and sugar, dissolve cocoa in the hot water, and mix the other ingredients well.—Mrs. Glenn Dunblazier, Minn.

Fruit Cake

1 lb. butter
1 lb. sugar
12 eggs
1 lb. flour
2 tsp. cinnamon
¾ tsp. nutmeg
¾ tsp. allspice

¾ tsp. mace
½ tsp. cloves
¾ c. cider
2 tsp. lemon juice
3 lb. seeded raisins
1 lb. currants
1 lb. citron (thinly sliced)

1 lb. figs (chopped fine)

Cream the butter, add sugar gradually and beat thoroly. Separate the yolks from the whites of eggs, beat yolks until thick and lemon colored. Beat the whites until stiff and dry and add to the first mixture. Add flour (excepting ⅓ c.) which should be reserved to dredge fruit, mixed and sifted with spices, add cider and lemon juice, then add fruit except citron, dredged with reserved flour. Dredge citron with flour and put in layers between cake mixture when putting in the pan. Bake 4 hr. in a very slow oven or steam 3 hr. and bake 1½ hr. in slow oven.—Mrs. Joe Abraham, N. D.

Love Cake

No. 1. ½ c. butter, 1 c. sugar. Mix until nearly white.
No. 2. Beat yolks of 3 eggs
No. 3. Add 1 c. sugar with beaten eggs.
No. 4. Add No. 1 with No. 3 and beat good.
No. 5. Put 2 c. of pastry flour and 2 tsp of baking powder in a sieve—sift half with ½ c. milk into the above mixture.
No. 6. Then add other half with another ½ c. milk.
No. 7. Beat whites of 3 eggs to stiff froth and add to above batter. Add flavor and pinch of salt. Bake in moderate oven.

—Mrs. R. L. McKee, Mich.

Banana Cake

1½ c. sugar
½ c. shortening
3 eggs
½ c. walnut meats
1 c. banana pulp

¼ c. sour milk
2 c. flour
½ tsp. salt
1 tsp. baking powder
1 tsp. soda

Cream butter and sugar. Add slightly beaten egg yolks and banana pulp. Add sour milk and nuts. Add flour with salt and baking powder sifted together. Lastly add well beaten whites, add soda dissolved in 1 tbsp. boiling water. Pour into well greased and floured pans. Bake in oven (350°) 12 min. Increase heat to (400°) for last part of baking, 30 min. Serve with sweetened whip cream or frost with favorite frosting.—Mrs. Frank Hoover, Canada.

Prune Cake

1 c. sugar
3 eggs
1 c. prune juice
1 c. raisins
½ tsp. cinnamon
2 c. flour

½ c. butter
1 c. stewed prunes (pitted)
1 c. chopped walnuts
¼ tsp. nutmeg
1 tsp. soda
1 tsp. baking powder

Cream together the sugar, butter and egg yolks then add prunes and spices then the flour, baking powder and soda, alternately with the prune juice, the raisins and walnuts and lastly fold in the beaten egg whites. Bake in moderate oven 30 min.—Mrs. Wm. H. Liefer, Minn.

Maple Nut Cake

½ c. butter
1½ c. brown sugar
2¼ c. cake flour
1 c. chopped walnut meats

¾ c. milk
1 tsp. maple flavoring
2 eggs
¼ tsp. salt

3 tsp. baking powder

Sift flour once before measuring, cream shortening, add sugar gradually, then beaten egg yolks. Then add flour sifted twice (putting baking powder in second sifting). Maple flavoring, salt and walnut meats. Lastly add whites of eggs beaten until stiff. Bake in angel food cake pan 45 min. in moderate oven (350°) in layer or 30 min. at (375°).—Mrs. N. S. Gashaw, Colo.

Spice Cake (sour cream)

2 eggs
1 c. sour cream
1¼ c. sugar
1 tsp. cinnamon
½ tsp. cloves

½ tsp. nutmeg
¼ tsp. salt
1¼ c. flour
1 tsp. soda
1 c. raisins

½ c. nutmeats

Beat eggs, add with sugar to sour cream. Sift the spices, soda and salt with flour. Add raisins and nuts. Bake for about 45 min. in moderate oven.—Mrs. B. C. Morris, S. Dak.

Potato Caramel Cake

4 eggs
2 c. sugar
2 c. flour
½ c. sweet milk
1 c. hot mashed potatoes
1 tsp. cloves

1 c. chopped nuts
2 tsp. baking powder
  (sifted with flour)
⅔ c. butter
1 c. grated chocolate
2 tsp. cinnamon

Cream sugar, butter and yolks of eggs and mix the chocolate with the potatoes Add the sugar and butter and yolks then the flour, add the beaten whites of eggs and last the nuts. You may add raisins sprinkled with ½ c. flour if desired. Bake in loaf pan in slow oven 45 min. If baked too long cake will be dry, otherwise, moist and delicious. Icing: Use 2½ c. brown sugar with water to dissolve it. Let boil until it makes a soft ball in cold water and pour over the well beaten whites of 3 eggs and flavor with vanilla and spread between layers and over the out side.—Mrs. Wm. E. Parker, Nebr.

Picnic Caramel Cake

½ c. butter or substitute	1 c. milk
1½ c. sugar	1 tsp. vanilla
4 tsp. baking powder	4 egg yolks beaten light
¼ tsp. salt	4 egg whites stiffly beaten
3 c. cake flour	

Cream the shortening with ¾ c. sugar, beat egg yolks until light and add remaining ¾ c. sugar, beating well. Add egg and sugar mixture to that of shortening and sugar mixing well. Sift flour, measure, add baking powder and salt, and sift three times. Add this flour mixture and milk alternately to the first mixture. Then add vanilla, fold in egg whites. Bake in layer cake pans in moderate oven (375°).—Mrs. Ivol E. Serrell, Ia.

Ice Box Cake

¾ lb. powdered sugar	¼ lb. candied cherries
½ lb. butter	Small can of crushed pine-
4 eggs	apple
1 pt. whipping cream	3 doz. lady fingers

Cream butter and sugar. Separate the eggs and add yolks, 1 at a time to the sugar mixture, beating well. Add beaten whites and vanilla. Line bottom of deep cake pan or angel food cake pan from which the tube has been removed, with paraffin paper. Split lady fingers and put layer in the bottom of the cake pan. Cover with ⅓ sugar mixture. Cover this with some of the cherries and pineapple. Whip 1 c. of the cream and spread ½ of this over the fruit. Then make another layer of the lady fingers and so on until all is used, saving enough of the sugar mixture for the top layer. Place in the ice box and allow to stand at least over night. Turn out from pan and cover with the other cup of whipping cream, beaten stiff and sweetened to taste. Decorate with cherries. Cut and serve as you would any cake.—Mrs. W. H. Hauser, S. Dak.

Chocolate Ice Box Cake

30 lady fingers or	4 eggs separated
left over cake strips	½ lb. sweet chocolate
½ pt. whipped cream	3 tbsp. water
3 tbsp. sugar	

Line the sides and bottom of a spring form or baking dish with the lady fingers or cake strips and put in the following filling: Melt chocolate in double boiler, add sugar and water with the yolks of the eggs well beaten. Cook slowly until thick and smooth, stirring constantly. When cool add the stiffly beaten whites of eggs. Cover lady fingers with a layer of this filling on top of this another layer of lady fingers, again some of the filling and so on depending on size of form with the lady fingers on top. Place in ice box 12 hrs. or more. When ready to serve remove to cake platter. Cover with whipping cream, add while whipping ¼ c. powdered sugar and ½ tsp. vanilla.—Mrs. Grest Ebel, Wis.

Chocolate Cake

2 c. flour	¼ tsp. soda
3 tsp. baking powder	2 eggs
½ tsp. salt	1½ c. sugar
⅓ c. cocoa	½ c. milk
½ c. water	1 tsp. vanilla

⅓ c. shortening

Cream the butter and sugar: Add beaten egg yolks and cocoa and water which has been cooked to a thin paste. Add dry ingredients and milk alternately and fold in beaten whites of eggs.—Mrs. Frank Hortin, Ill.

Spanish Chocolate Cake

1 c. sugar	2½ c. flour
½ c. sweet milk	1 tsp. baking powder
½ c. butter	2 eggs

1 tsp. soda dissolved in 2 tbsp. hot water

Part 2: Melt 3 oz. chocolate over hot water, stir in 1 c. sugar, yolk of 1 egg and 1 c. milk. Stir until thick and then cool. Flavor with vanilla.

Cream butter and sugar, add egg yolks well beaten and milk alternately with flour which has been sifted with baking powder, add soda and chocolate mixture. Lastly fold in egg whites. Bake in moderate oven in two layers (375°).—Elizabeth Dachtler, S. Dak.

Chocolate Roll Cake

6 eggs	2 tbsp. cocoa
½ c. sugar	1 c. flour

Beat egg yolks light and add sugar. Add the cocoa, flour and stiffly beaten whites of egg. Grease pan well, put in the dough and bake 10 min. in hot oven. Sprinkle sugar on towel and place cake on it. When cool spread with whipped cream and roll like a jelly roll. May be served with whipped cream or sauce made of the following: 1 c. sugar, ½ c. milk, ¼ c.

cocoa, 1 tbsp. butter, little water, 1 tbsp. corn starch. Cook until thick.—Grace Montgomery, Mo.

Angel Food Cake

Before starting to bake angel food cake sift the sugar twice and the flour 4 times. Measure the flour after it has been sifted once.

1¼ c. egg whites	1 tsp. cream tartar
¼ tsp. salt	1 c. cake flour
1½ c. granulated sugar	1 tsp. vanilla
¼ tsp. almond	

Place egg whites in large platter or crock, add salt, beat with a whisk egg beater until frothy. Add cream tartar, continue beating till eggs are stiff but not dry, fold in sugar 1 tbsp at a time. Add flavoring, fold flour in the same way as sugar. Pour in ungreased angel food pan, bake in slow oven (300°) 50 to 60 min. increasing the heat slightly when cake is almost done. Remove cake from oven, invert pan for 1 hr. remove from pan with a spatula.—Mrs. Chas. Klein, Ill.

Fruit Cake (White)

4 c. cake flour	1 lb. blanched almonds
1 tsp. baking powder	(cut fine)
½ tsp. soda	½ lb. each candied pine-
½ tsp. salt	apple, orange and
1 c. shortening	lemon peel and mara-
1½ c. granulated sugar	chino cherries
1 tbsp lemon juice	10 egg whites stiffly
1 lb. Sultana raisins	beaten
½ lb. citron, cut fine	

Sift flour once, add dry ingredients and sift 5 times, sift 1 c. of the flour mixture over fruit and nuts, mix well. Cream butter and sugar, add flour mixture small amount at a time, add lemon juice, fruit and nuts, fold in egg whites. Bake in slow oven 2½ hr.—Mrs. Minnie Williams, Ohio.

Lemon Cake

½ c. butter	2 c. flour
1½ c. sugar	2 tsp. baking powder
¾ c. water	1 tsp. lemon
3 eggs	

Cream butter and sugar until fluffy, add water and the 2 c. flour which have been sifted with the baking powder, add lemon. Divide this mixture into two equal parts, add the beaten yolks of eggs to 1 portion and the stiffly beaten whites in the other portion. Bake in two layers in quick oven (400°) and put together with the following filling: 2 tbsp. butter mixed with 2 c. confectioners sugar, the juice of ½ lemon and the rind of 1 whole lemon. If not of proper consistency to spread add cream.—Mrs. L. F. Thornton, Wyo.

Prince of Wales Cake

½ c. shortening
1½ c. brown sugar
2 eggs
2 c. pastry flour
½ tsp. each baking pow-
der, soda, cloves, all-
spice
1 tsp. nutmeg
2 tsp. ginger
¾ c. sour milk

Cream shortening, slowly add sugar until mixture is fluffy. Add beaten yolks of eggs, sift dry ingredients together, add to the creamed shortening sugar and egg yolks alternately with ¾ c. sour milk. Lastly fold in the stiffly beaten whites of the eggs. Bake in two layers in a moderate oven (375°) for 25 min. Ice with the following: 2 c. confectioners sugar, 4 tbsp. butter, add boiling water a little at a time until butter is softened, then thin to the proper consistency with cream, flavor with ½ tsp. each of vanilla and lemon, add 1 c. raisins cut fine.—Mabel House, Kansas.

Moonlight Cake

10 eggs (whites only)
7 egg yolks
½ tsp. salt
1½ c. sugar (sift 5 times)
1 c. cake flour (sift 5 times
⅞ tsp. cream tartar
1 tsp. flavoring

Beat egg whites until frothy and then add cream tartar; continue beating until egg whites are stiff but not dry. In another bowl beat the 7 egg yolks until creamy and add to them 2 tbsp. of beaten whites. To the whites add gradually the sifted sugar; now combine the yellow and white mixtures and add the flour and flavoring. Bake in an angel food pan, rinsing the pan with cold water before putting in the batter. Bake in a very slow oven, (like angel food). This makes a large, dainty cake.—Mrs. R. H. Hiles, Mo.

Mrs. Moody's Wonder Cake

Cream ½ c. butter with 1½ c. powdered sugar. Add alternately a little at a time ½ c. milk and 2 c. flour with which 2 tsp. baking powder has been sifted, 1 tsp. vanilla, lastly fold in 6 egg whites beaten. Bake in 3 layer tins.—Mrs. Wesley Tabaka, N. Dak.

Spanish Bun Cake

1¼ c. brown sugar
1 tbsp. butter
2 egg yolks
½ tsp. soda dissolved
1 c. sour cream
1 c. raisins
½ c. nut meats
1 tsp. vanilla
¼ tsp. nutmeg
1¾ c. flour
Add whites of 2 eggs beaten stiff

Cream sugar and butter until fluffy. Add yolks of eggs and beat hard. Add cream with soda dissolved then add raisins, nut meats, vanilla, and nutmeg. Then add flour and beat thoroly, adding the beaten egg whites. Bake in moderate oven (350°) for 45 min. in loaf.—Mrs. Tillye C. Burchard, Ill.

Pound Cake

Have utensils and material cold. If it is warm weather place mixing bowl in pan of ice water. Measure 1 c. of butter and break in small pieces in mixing bowl. Work butter with a wooden spoon until it becomes soft as cold cream. You cannot beat it too much. Measure 1½ c. sifted pastry flour and sift again ¾ tsp. baking powder, ¼ tsp. salt, ¼ tsp. mace. Sift this mixture into the creamed butter a little at a time constantly working the butter to keep it in a creamy condition. When all the flour has been added give it another good beating. Meanwhile select 5 eggs of uniform size, separate yolks from whites. Beat yolks until they are thick and cream colored. Add to this 1⅓ c. of sifted confectioners sugar a little at a time until it is all added. Then add egg yolk mixture to butter and flour beating constantly. Beat egg whites until they are stiff and dry. Fold them into the cake and then contrary to the usual method when beaten whites are used, beat the mixture until it resembles a hard sauce with no trace of egg apparent. Add ½ tsp. vanilla and pour at once into paper lined cake pan and bake from 1 to 1¼ hr. Test with a straw to make sure it is done. This cake may be varied by adding a cup of nuts or citron, finely chopped to the flour mixture before combining with the egg mixture. Bake at (350°).— Mrs. Joe Diehn, Wis.

Bakeless Cake

3 egg yolks
½ c. sugar
½ c. melted butter
1 c. crushed pineapple or banana

1 c. nut meats
1 c. cocoanut
¼ lb. vanilla wafers

Beat egg yolks until lemon colored. Add sugar and beat again. Add melted butter and cream all together thoroly. Add fruit and nuts. Place vanilla wafers in bottom of baking dish. Add a layer of batter. Alternately add wafers and batter until ingredients are used. Set in a cold place to harden for 24 hr. Slice and serve with whip cream.—Mrs. W. J. Longmore, Nebr.

Apple Sauce Cake

½ lb. shortening
1 c. brown sugar
1 egg
1½ c. flour
1 c. raisins

1 tsp. each soda, cinnamon, salt, cloves
1 c. unsweetened apple sauce

Cream shortening and brown sugar, add beaten egg, apple sauce and raisins. Sift dry ingredients and add to above mixture. Bake in loaf, in moderate oven 45 min.—Mrs. Earl Brossard, Minn.

Hickory Nut Cake

Cream ¾ c. butter and 2 c. light brown sugar. Add 1 c. cold water, 4 egg yolks well beaten, ½ tsp. ground cinnamon and mace, 3 c. flour into which has been sifted 3 tsp. baking powder, ½ tsp. salt, 4 egg whites beaten stiff, 2 blanched hickory nut meats chopped fine. Roll in flour, add gradually to mixture stirring all the time. Pour in loaf cake tin, cover with browned flour first ½ hr. or oiled paper. Let bake 1 hr. When cool turn out of tin, cover with boiled icing and decorate with whole nut kernels.—Mrs. W. B. Little, Ill.

Butterscotch Cocoanut Layer Cake

1½ c. flour
2 tsp. baking powder
1 egg
1 tsp. lemon or vanilla ext.

⅞ c. sugar
2 tsp. shortening
½ c. milk
½ c. grated cocoanut

Sift flour, sugar and baking powder. Add melted shortening and beaten eggs to milk and add dry ingredients. Mix well and add flavoring and cocoanut. Bake in three layers and use the following filling: Blend thoroly 2 c. light brown sugar with 4 level tbsp. flour. Well beaten yolks of 3 eggs and 2 tbsp. butter; place in double boiler. Add slowly 1 c. scalded milk and cook 7 to 10 min. stirring constantly. When cool add 1 tsp. vanilla, 1 tbsp. cream and ½ can Bakers cocoanut (put through food chopper).

Icing: Cook together 1½ c. brown sugar, ½ c. water, 2 tbsp. butter, 1 tsp. vanilla till it forms a soft ball when dropped in water. Beat till it is of right consistency to spread over tops and sides of cake and cover with cocoanut.—Mrs. Lynn Beecher, Texas.

Crumb Cake

3 c. flour
2 c. brown sugar
1 c. butter or lard
Mix like pie crust and take out 1 c. mixture then to rest add

2 eggs
1 c. sour milk
1 tsp. soda
1 tsp. cinnamon
½ tsp. cloves

Beat hard put in loaf cake pan and sprinkle 1 c. of crumbs, saved out of top. Bake 40 min. in slow oven. Instead of using butter or lard 1c. of sour cream can be used. This makes it nourishing for young and old.—Ella Teetzen, Kansas.

Coffee Cake

1 c. brown sugar
1 c. butter
2 eggs
1 tsp. cloves
1 tsp. cinnamon
1 c. walnuts
1 c. coffee
1 c. raisins
2½ c. flour and 1 tsp. soda (sifted together)

Cream butter and sugar and eggs until well blended, add spices and soda to flour and sift well, add cold coffee to the creamed mixture, add flour and spices then raisins and chopped walnut meats. Bake in a moderate oven.—Inzie M. Bean, N. Dak.

Burnt Sugar Cake

½ c. butter
1½ c. sugar
2½ c. flour
1 c. cold water
1 tsp. vanilla
2 tsp. baking powder
3 tsp. burnt sugar
2 eggs

Cream butter and sugar, add egg yolks and water, beat well. Sift flour and baking powder, add to mixture with vanilla, burnt sugar, and stiffly beaten egg whites. Beat well and bake in layers in moderate oven.—Nova Sanders, Mo.

Brown Stone Front Cake

½ c. butter
1½ c. sugar
½ c. cocoa
½ c. sweet milk
½ c. hot water
2 eggs
1 tsp. soda
2 c. flour

Cream butter and sugar. Dissolve cocoa in hot water and add eggs beaten, add milk and flavoring. Dissolve soda in hot water, add flour. This makes a splendid cake and is a rich mahogany color.—Mrs. Harry Atzen, Ia.

Buttermilk Cake

2 c. sugar
¾ c. butter or lard
2 c. buttermilk
4 c. flour sifted with following:
1 tsp. soda, cinnamon, allspice
½ tsp. cloves
2 tbsp. cocoa
1 c. seeded raisins

Mix as for any cake. Bake in moderate oven.—Mrs. H. A. Lutcavish, Nebr.

Greenapple Cake

1 c. sugar
½ c. butter
2 eggs
1 c. green apples chopped
½ c. nuts
½ c. raisins
1 c. strong coffee
1½ c. flour
1 tsp. each soda, cinnamon, nutmeg and allspice

Mix sugar and butter, add egg yolks and chopped apples, next add nuts and raisins, sift dry ingredients and add alternately with coffee to butter mixture. Lastly fold in whites of eggs beaten stiff. Bake in moderate oven (375°).—Mrs. Martin Larson, N. Dak.

Angel Food Cake (improved)

Whites of 13 large eggs
1¼ c. sugar
1 c. cake flour
1 heaping tsp. cream tartar
1 tsp. any preferred ext.
Juice of 1 lemon
½ c. coarsely chopped pecans
1½ slices pineapple
12 marachino cherries

Cut cherries and pineapple in small pieces. Beat egg whites until stiff then add cream of tartar, beat again and then fold in sugar. Add extract and lemon juice and fold this well into mixture. Then fold in flour lightly and add nuts and fruit last. Bake in a moderate oven about 1 hr. Test with straw.—Mrs. Chas. Couch, Mo.

Cherry Cake

1½ c. sugar
½ c. butter
2 eggs
1 c. cherries (cooked and
pitted)
1 c. sour milk
Cinnamon and nutmeg
1 tsp. soda
2 c. flour

Mix same as other cakes, ice with powdered sugar frosting.—Mrs. Alva Brown, Calif.

Potato Fudge Cake

1 c. butter
½ tsp. allspice, cloves and cinnamon (each)
2 c. sugar
4 eggs beaten separately
1 c. grated raw potatoes
1 bar sweet chocolate
Grated rind of 1 lemon
½ c. sweet milk
2¼ c. cake flour
2¼ tsp. baking powder
½ lb. chopped almonds

Cream shortening, add sugar gradually then the beaten egg yolks and potatoes. Sift flour and add dry ingredients and lemon rind, use parts of flour to dust nut meats and add milk and dry ingredients alternately then the melted chocolate and fold in the egg whites last. Bake in a round cake tin in a moderate oven about 1 hr.—Mrs. Bernard Pieper, Ill.

Graham Cracker Cake

½ c. butter
1 c. sugar
3 egg yolks
¾ c. milk
1 lb graham cracker
    crumbs

2 tsp. baking powder
1 tsp. vanilla
1 c. chopped nuts
3 egg whites

Combine sugar, butter and eggs and add cracker crumbs rolled fine, and baking powder. Add nuts and vanilla. The well beaten whites are folded in last. Bake in loaf or 2 layers. —Mrs. T. A. Sinz, Wis.

Jam Cake

5 eggs
2 c. sugar
2 c. jam
1 c. buttermilk
1 c. butter

4 c. flour
2 tsp. nutmeg
1 tsp. cinnamon
1 tsp. cloves
1 tsp. soda

1 tsp. baking powder

Mix butter and sugar, add jam, and egg yolks thoroly beaten. Sift dry ingredients and add alternately with buttermilk to butter mixture.—Mrs. Gertrude Watson, Mo.

Pork Cake

1 lb. salt pork
2 c. boiling water
2 c. dark brown sugar
1 c. dark cooking syrup
1 tsp. soda
1 lb. raisins

1 lb. chopped dates
¼ lb. shredded citron
4 c. flour
1 tsp. cinnamon
1 tsp. cloves
1 tsp. allspice

1 tsp. nutmeg

Chop pork fine, pour over it the boiling water, add sugar and syrup, stir in fruit and add flour well blended with spices. Mix thoroly and bake in individual bread pans in quite a moderate oven (350°). Will keep indefinitely if stored in tight container and not frosted. Any good boiled white icing is nice when ready to serve.—Mrs. P. S. Hair, Minn.

Pineapple Cake

Cream ½ c. butter and 1 c. sugar. Beat in 3 well beaten eggs. Add 1½ c. flour with 2 tsp. baking powder and ¼ tsp. soda sifted with flour. Stir, then add 1 c. grated pineapple and stir again. This makes 2 layers. Bake in moderate oven (350°) 30 min.—Mrs. Arthur Winkler, Kansas.

Sponge Cake Using Egg Yolks Only

6 egg yolks
1 c. sugar
½ c. boiling water
1 tsp. lemon extract
½ tsp. salt
2 tsp. baking powder
1½ c. flour

Beat egg yolks until light with a Dover beater. Add sugar gradually then hot water beating meanwhile. Add flour sifted with baking powder and salt and beat thoroly. Bake in loaf in moderate oven (350°) about 45 min. or in 2 layers hot oven (375°) 25 min. Put layers together with cream filling.—Mrs. Oscar Rippee, Idaho.

Sponge Cake

Beat stiff the whites of 5 eggs, add slowly ½ c. granulated sugar. Beat until quite stiff. Beat the yolks of eggs stiff and add ⅓ c. sugar and beat well. Fold the whites and yolks together, add ½ tsp. vanilla. Sift in slowly 1 c. of pastry flour sifted with ½ tsp. baking powder and ¼ tsp. salt. Fold flour in lightly. Bake 30 to 40 min. in medium hot oven (350°). This never fails and is splendid.—Mrs. Wm. Pugh, Ohio.

Spice Cake

1½ c. brown sugar
½ c. butter
1 egg
Mix well and add:
1 c. sour milk
1 tsp. soda dissolved in
    sour milk
Stir well and add:
1 tsp. vanilla
¼ tsp. cloves
½ tsp. nutmeg
1 tsp. cinnamon
2 c. flour
½ c. raisins
½ c. nutmeats

Mix well and bake in a moderate oven (350°).—Mrs. John Carlett, Ia.

Boiled Spice Cake

2 c. sugar
2 c. water
2 c. raisins
¾ c. lard or butter
1 tsp. salt
2 tsp. cinnamon
½ tsp. cloves
Put in kettle and let boil, cool and add:
2 well beaten eggs
2 tsp. soda
3 c. flour sifted with
    2 tsp. baking powder

Bake 1 hr. in moderate oven (350°).—S. Covault, Kansas.

Whipped Cream Cake

1 c. sweet whipped cream
1 c. sugar
2 eggs
½ tsp. salt
1 tsp. vanilla
2 tsp. baking powder
.... 1½ c. flour

Whip cream until firm. Drop in eggs and whip until light as foam. Add sugar and beat again. Add salt and vanilla. Whip in flour and baking powder put in layer cake tins and bake in rather quick oven. Frost with boiled icing and cover with cocoanut. Delicious.—Muriel Martin, Mont.

Sour Cream Cake

Break 1 egg in a cup and fill with sour cream. Pour in mixing bowl, beat well and add 1 c. brown sugar.

1½ c. flour	½ tsp. soda
¼ tsp. salt	½ tsp. baking powder

½ tsp. cinnamon

Mix salt, soda, baking powder, cinnamon with the flour and sift three times then stir in the other ingredients and bake in a small loaf tin in a moderate oven. Ice with lemon icing made with powdered sugar and lemon juice.—Miss Lizzie Coyan, Ia.

FROSTING

Yellow Jacket Icing

Boil

1½ c. sugar

½ c. water

2 tbsp. dark syrup until it threads

2 egg yolks add to syrup

Beat in marshmallows. Continue beating until it piles.—Mrs. Everett Cline, North Dakota.

Cake Filling

Bake any favorite white cake, layer, when cold, put between the following filling:

2 sour apples, grated

4 egg yolks

Butter size of walnut

1 c. sugar (scant)

Grated rind and juice of 1 orange or lemon. Cook until thick. When cool put between layers. A smaller number of yolks may be used and flour or cornstarch may be substituted.—Mrs. Maye Hoff, Arkansas.

Orange Frosting

Grated rind of 1 orange

½ tsp. lemon juice

1 tbsp. orange juice

1½ c. confectioner's sugar

yolk of 1 egg

Add the rind to fruit juices and let stand 15 min. Strain, and add gradually to yolk of egg slightly beaten. Stir in sugar until of right consistency to spread.—Mrs. M. C. Hoxie, California.

Comfort Icing

2½ c. sugar

½ c. syrup (white)

½ c. water

2 egg whites

Boil sugar, syrup and water 1 min., then slowly add 3 tbsp. of the stiffly beaten egg whites. Cook remainder until a soft ball is formed, add all but 1 c. Cook this till a hard ball is formed and add to egg whites, beat until cool. This may be put on cake at once or kept in a covered jar. It keeps 2 weeks (much longer than that in cold weather). When putting it on a cake add enough warm water to thin enough to spread.—Mrs. L. F. Thornton, Wyoming.

Cake Icing

1 c. sugar

1 c. sour cream

2 tbsp. butter

Cook until it thickens, then beat until stiff to spread. It will not crack off no matter how long you cook it.—Mrs Lillie Bontrager, Missouri.

Uncooked Ormamental Icing

Beat:
3 eggs until foamy, add
1 tsp. cream tartar

Gradually add
1 lb. 4x sugar
1 tsp. flavoring and beat
long and hard

Color any color desired or divide and color all. A real time and labor saver.—Pearl E. Pearson, Arizona.

Cake Frosting

(Never Fails)

Boil together 1 c. sugar and 4 tbsp. water and 1 level tsp. cornstarch and ¼ tsp. cream tartar. Boil to the soft ball stage when tested in cold water. Beat slowly into the stiffly beaten white of 1 egg. Flavor to taste. To vary this, one may add while mixture is boiling, 4 tsp. sugar that has been caramelized by browning. This will produce a caramel frosting. For variety add chopped nuts or shredded cocoanut to the white frosting or make the frosting with brown instead of white sugar, and to make chocolate frosting, add 3 tsp. cocoa to the boiling mixture.—Mrs. Walter Whanger, Missouri.

Cake Filling

1 c. sugar
2 tbsp. S. D. flour
Grated rind 1 orange
½ c. orange juice

3 tbsp. lemon juice
4 tbsp. water
1 egg slightly beaten
2 tsp. butter

Mix ingredients in order given. Cook 10 min. in a double boiler, stirring constantly. Cool before spreading.—Miss Myrtle E. Jorgens, South Dakota.

7 Minute Frosting

2 egg whites
1½ c. sugar

5 tbsp. cold water
¼ tsp. cream tartar

1 tsp. vanilla

Put egg whites, sugar, water, and cream tartar in upper part of a double boiler. Beat with rotary egg beater until thoroughly mixed. Place over rapid boiling water, beat constantly, and cook for 7 min. or until frosting will stand in peaks. Remove from fire, add vanilla and beat until thick enough to spread. Spread between layer and on top and sides of cake. Sprinkle each layer and outside of cake with cocoanut while frosting is still soft.—Mrs. Chas. Oakes, North Dakota.

Orange Frosting

2 egg yolks
5 tbsp. orange juice
1 tbsp. grated orange rind

1 tsp. lemon juice
2 c. powdered sugar

Mix orange and lemon juice with rind and let stand 10 min. Then strain it and add to egg yolks, slowly add powdered sugar and beat until of the right consistency to spread.—Mrs. O. A. Fergerson, Texas.

COOKIES

Yum Yums

1 c. flour
1 c. chopped dates
1 c. chopped nuts
1 c. sugar

⅓ c. sweet milk
1 egg
1 pinch salt
2 tsp. baking powder

Beat egg until thick and lemon colored, add sugar, beat again, mix dry ingredients with flour, add milk, fruit and nuts. —Mary C. Fitzgerald, South Dakota.

Ginger Snaps

1 c. sugar
½ c. butter or lard
Mix well
1 egg

Pinch of salt
1 tbsp. soda, dissolved in
1 c. molasses
1 tbsp. ginger

3½ c. flour

Mix the dough until sticky. Roll out with hands, forming them with the hands, leaving ½ inch thick, which makes them crack on top. Do not form your cookies very large, for they raise when in oven. Leave them quite far apart. You can also make other kinds of cookies this way, by adding syrup instead of molasses, or omitting the ginger and molasses and put crystal white syrup in and add vanilla. Roll them in sugar before baking. Bake in hot oven.—Alma Wille, North Dakota.

Oat Meal Cookies

1 c. butter or lard (scant)
1 c. sugar
1¾ c. oatmeal
2 eggs
5 tbsp. sour milk

1 small tsp. soda
1 c. raisins
1 tsp. cinnamon
1 c. flour
½ tsp. salt

Cream shortening, add sugar, egg well beaten, mix soda with sour milk, add oatmeal, flour, fruit and salt. Drop from teaspoon. Bake in moderate oven.—Miss Hazel E. Pearson, Kansas.

Delicious Filled Cookies

For filling:
1 c. raisins
1 c. boiling water

⅔ c. sugar
1 tbsp. flour boiled until
    thick

Set aside to cool

For Dough:
½ c. lard
1 c. sugar
½ c. milk

1 egg
1 tsp. vanilla
3 tsp. baking powder

Enough flour to make a medium dough. Roll out thin and cut in any desired shape. Put a layer of the filling between 2 cookies, press edges together lightly and bake in a hot oven.—Mrs. A. C. Simmons, Missouri.

Spiced Raisin Cookies

½ c. raisins	1 egg
⅓ c. butter	1¾ c. flour
⅔ c. sugar	½ tsp. cinnamon
3 tbsp. milk	⅓ tsp. salt
2 tsp. baking powder	¼ tsp. cloves
¼ tsp. nutmeg	

Cream butter and sugar, add well beaten egg, sift flour with dry ingredients. Add to butter and sugar mixture, beat in raisins. Drop from a teasoon. Bake in hot oven.—Mrs. Hans. Kallesen, Iowa.

Orange Cookies

⅔ c. butter	Juice of 2 oranges
1⅔ c. sugar	Grated rind of 2 oranges
2 eggs	3 tsp. baking powder
4½ c. flour	

Cream the butter and sugar and add beaten eggs and juice and rind of oranges. Measure baking powder, add to sifted flour and combine with other ingredients, roll thin and bake in a quick but not too hot oven. By the use of lemons, instead of oranges, one may make delightful lemon cookies from this recipe. These cookies are very crisp and excellent for school lunches or to serve with tea.—Mrs. Elsie Barclay, Kansas.

Raspberry Cookies

3 c. sifted flour	Grated rind of 1 lemon
2½ tsp. baking powder	1 egg (beaten light)
¼ tsp. salt	¼ c. milk
½ c. butter	½ lb. raspberry jam
1 c. sugar	1 egg (white)
More sugar	

Sift together three times the flour, baking powder and salt. Cream butter, add sugar, grated rind, egg and alternately the milk and flour mixture. Knead in the last of the flour mixture. Roll the dough (part at a time) into a thin sheet and cut into rounds. Spread half the rounds nearly to the edge with jam; lay the other half over the jam and press together lightly; set into a baking pan, brush over the tops with white of egg, dredge with granulated sugar and bake about 12 min.—Mrs. Hal A. Waisner, Kansas.

Honey Cookies

1 c. shortening
1 c. brown sugar
2 c. honey
3 eggs (beaten)
Flour

½ c. coffee
1 tbsp. soda
2 tsp. baking powder
1 tsp. ginger
¼ tsp. salt

Cream the shortening, add sugar, beaten eggs and honey, and mix and sift about 3 c. flour with the dry ingredients and add alternately with the coffee to the first mixture. Add enough more sifted flour to roll. Chill the dough a little and it will be much more easily handled. Do not roll too thin. Cut and bake in a moderately hot oven.—Mrs. Boyd K. Wassmann, Minnesota.

Sugar Cookies

2 c. sugar
1 c. butter or shortening
1 tsp. soda

3 eggs
1 c. sour cream

Season with cinnamon or lemon extract. Add just enough flour so cookies will roll without sticking. Handle as little as possible.—Mrs. Lloyd Place, Milford, Iowa.

Sugar Cookies

2 c. sugar
2 c. butter (scant)

Cream well
4 eggs (beaten very light)

To butter and sugar add eggs, and cream this. 2 tbsp. cold water, 1 tsp. vanilla, and add to the other mixture. 2 tsp. baking powder, sifted with flour and add flour enough for a medium soft dough. Roll out very thin and bake in a quick oven. These will keep fine for weeks.—Mrs. S. J. Houge, Minnesota.

Chocolate Cream Cookies

1½ c. sugar
2 tbsp. butter
1 tbsp. lard
Beat to a cream
Add:
1 egg beaten
½ c. cocoa mixed smooth
    with either hot water
    or coffee

Which has added:
1 tsp. soda
1 c. sour cream
1 tsp. vanilla
3 c. sifted flour
Which has added:
1 tsp. salt
1 tsp. cinnamon
7 level tsp. baking powder

Drop on greased and floured pans with a teaspoon. Bake in quick oven. Frost with cream frosting. Dough must be just stiff enough so that when they bake they spread out flat and even as cookies. Frosting as follows: Boil together: 1½ c. sugar; ½ c. rich milk till it begins to thicken. Take from fire and add: 1 tsp. butter; 1 tsp. vanilla; spread when cool and thick.—Mrs. Oscar Haugen, Wisconsin.

Cocoanut Cookies

2 c. butter or shortening	1 c. cocoanut
2 c. sugar	2 tsp. vanilla
3 c. flour	1 tsp. soda
4 eggs	2 tsp. cream tartar

Cream butter and add sugar and vanilla. Beat the eggs and add to the butter and sugar. Sift the soda and cream tartar together and also sift them with the flour. Mix cocoanut with flour and mix all together. Drop in tins and bake.—Mrs. Sam Lichte, Kansas.

Macaroons

4 egg whites beaten stiff	1 c. white sugar
1 c. chopped walnuts	1 c. cocoanut
3 c. corn flakes	

Mix and bake on buttered sheet in hot oven.—Mrs. W. B. Nunn, North Dakota.

Butter Scotch Cookies

1 c. nuts	3½ c. flour
2 c. brown sugar	1 tsp. soda
1 c. butter	1 tsp. cream tartar
3 eggs	1 tsp. salt
1 tsp. vanilla	

Cream butter and sugar, add eggs. Sift flour with soda, cream of tartar and salt and nuts, mold into rolls and let stand over night in ice box. Slice off thin and bake.—Mrs. Geo. Beckman, Minnesota.

Overnight Cookies

1 c. sugar	5 c. flour
1 c. brown sugar	1 tsp. soda
1 c. lard	1 c. nuts
3 eggs beaten light	1 tsp. cinnamon and salt
Dissolve soda in a little hot water	

Mix at night, mold into loaves. In the morning slice thin and bake in hot oven.—Mrs. W. F. Puppe, North Dakota.

PASTRIES

A few cautions for the pastry maker. If making pie crust by the cold water method, be sure to have ingredients cold. If using the hot water method, have water boiling. Do not handle the dough. The more it is handled the more rubbery and tough it becomes. In making meringue, beat the egg whites stiff, add 2 tbsp. sugar for every egg white. Pile lightly on the pie and brown in an oven with a moderate temperature. It should take at least 15 min. to brown the meringue. This slow cooking will prevent a watery or tough meringue.

Date Pie

Line a pie tin with rich pastry and fill with the following:

1 c. walnut meats
1 c. dates
1 c. rich milk

¾ c. sugar
3 eggs
Salt

Mix beaten eggs, salt, sugar, and add milk, nuts and dates and bake in moderate oven till firm. Cool, serve with whipped cream.—Mrs. Frank Copp, Minnesota.

Prune Cream Pie

Stew slowly ½ lb. prunes which have been soaked overnight. Stone and press prunes thru colander. To a cup of pulp add 1 c. thin cream or rich milk. Mix 1 tsp. cornstarch with ⅓ c. sugar, add the yolks of 2 well beaten eggs and 1 tsp. vanilla. Line a pie plate with good pastry, fill with prune mixture and bake quickly. Beat the white of the eggs stiff, add 2 tbsp. granulated sugar, spread over the pie, return to the oven which must be slow and brown lightly.—Mrs. Hallie Abbott, Missouri.

"O So Good" Pie

1 c. brown sugar
1 tbsp. butter
2 eggs

½ tsp. cinnamon
½ tsp. cloves
½ c. raisins

½ c. nuts

Cream together, sugar, butter, egg yolks, cinnamon and cloves; add nuts and raisins, fold in the egg whites, beaten very

stiff. Cook in one crust, in a moderate oven 45 min. Serve
with whipped cream.—Miss Ruth Smedley, Arkansas.

Butterscotch Pie

¾ c. dark brown sugar   2 tbsp. flour (heaping)
2 egg yolks   1½ c. milk
2 tbsp. butter   1 tsp. vanilla

Cook in double boiler until it forms a custard. Use white of
eggs for meringue, adding 2 tbsp. sugar. Beat stiff and place
in the oven to brown.—Miss Hazel Brown, Iowa.

Fluff Pie

1 pt. fruit, either fresh or canned. Strawberries, raspberries or bananas if preferred. Break fruits into parts but do
not crush. Bake a rich crust. Whip the whites of 4 eggs very
stiff and add 4 tbsp. sugar. Whip again and add 4 tbsp. more
of sugar. Fold in the fruit, being careful not to crush too
much. Leave the top of filling in uneven ridges and bake in
oven 15 min.—Mrs. Flora Helbert, Indiana.

Washington Pie

½ c. sugar   4 tbsp. water
1 egg   ½ c. flour
large tsp. baking powder
Bake and cool and serve with following filling:
½ c. sugar   1 c. milk
1 tsp. vanilla   1 egg

Cook and thicken. When cool put between piece of the split
cake and on top. Garnish with whipped cream.—Mrs. Arthur
Pfolsgrof, Illinois.

Pecan Pie

Brown 1 c. sugar and 2 tbsp. flour; then add 1 c. boiling
sweet milk and stir until sugar dissolves. As you take from
stove add 1 tbsp. butter. When cool, add the well beaten yolks
of 2 eggs, ½ c. sweet milk, 1 c. pecans and 1 tsp. vanilla. Replace on stove and let thicken a little more if needed. Pour
into baked crust, cover with meringue. If desired, beat 2 egg
whites stiff and add 1½ tbsp. sugar and ½ tsp. baking powder,
let brown slightly.—Loraine Deaver, Texas.

Grape Pie (Concord)

Remove seed, run pulp thru a sieve, and add hulls:
1 c. grapes   2 egg yolks
¾ c. sugar   1 tbsp. butter

Bake in 1 crust and when done add meringue made with the
2 egg whites.—Mrs. T. B. Hayes, Texas.

Chocolate Cream Pie

1 c. milk	6 tbsp. sugar
1 c. water	1 square chocolate
2 eggs	¼ tsp. salt
4 tbsp. flour	1 tsp. vanilla

Mix flour, sugar, slat, and grated chocolate with a little of the diluted milk, then add yolks of eggs well beaten. Scald remainder of ·diluted milk, pour slowly on mixture, and cook in double boiler until it thickens, stirring constantly. Cool, flavor and pour into the pie shell, previously baked. Cover with stiffly beaten whites of eggs to which a tbsp. of confectioners sugar had been added. Brown lightly in oven.—Agnes Dixon, Maryland.

Blueberry Pie

1 qt. blueberries	3 tbsp. cream
¼ c. sugar	1 egg yolk
2 tbsp. lemon juice	Pinch of cinnamon

Cornstarch or flour

Line a pie tin with pastry and fill with the above filling and bake between 2 crusts.—Mrs. Lema Schendel, Minnesota.

Cranberry Pie

1¼ c. chopped cranberries	1 tbsp. flour
¾ c. chopped raisins	1 c. sugar
1 c. hot water	1 tsp. vanilla

Mix flour and sugar and pour hot water gradually over, stirring smooth and add the fruit chopped and cook a few min. Partly cool and flavor and fill crust, cover with strips of dough and bake.—Mrs. E. L. Behrens, Minnesota.

Sour Cream Pie

1 c. sour cream	1 tbsp. flour
2 egg yolks	¼ tsp. cinnamon
1 c. sugar	¼ tsp. cloves
1 c. raisins	Pinch of salt

Bake with 1 or 2 crusts. If you use sweet cream use 1 tsp. vinegar.—Mrs. Burton Morgan, Iowa.

Sunkist Lemon Pie

1 c. sugar	1 tsp. salt
1½ c. boiling water	2 eggs
3 tbsp. cornstarch	Grated rind of 1 lemon
3 tbsp. flour	½ c. lemon juice

Sift dry ingredients. Add water, cook in double boiler until thick, 15 min. Add slightly beaten egg yolks and cook 2 min. longer. Then add lemon juice and grated rind. Cool and turn into baked pie shell. Cover with meringue made by beating the egg whites until frothy adding 4 tbsp. sugar and ¼ tsp. baking powder and continue beating until stiff. Put into moderate oven (325 degrees) for 15 min. to brown.—Mrs. E. W. Howe, Kansas.

Lemon Whip Pie

3 eggs
1 c. sugar

4 tbsp. lemon juice
Grated rind of 1 lemon

Beat the yellows till very light and add ½ the sugar. Cook till thick. When cool add the juice of grated rind to the egg whites beaten stiff. Add the other ½ c. sugar and fold in the yellows.—Mrs. Ella Green, Illinois.

Banana Pie

Bake with one crust. Bake pie crust first, when cool take 2 large bananas, and slice them. Lay on pie crust. Beat the yolks of 2 eggs to a cream and 2 c. milk, ½ c. sugar, 2 tbsp. flour, and a small piece of butter. Pinch of salt. Boil till a good stiff custard and let cool. Spread over bananas and beat whites of 2 eggs with sugar. Spread on pie. Put in oven to brown.—Mrs. Homer Wheeler, Colorado.

Cocoanut Pie

1 pt. milk
3 eggs well beaten
1 c. sugar

1 c. shredded cocoanut
1 tsp. vanilla or nutmeg
Pinch of salt

Enough of this filling for either 2 small pies or 1 large one. —Mrs. C. W. Shaffer, Minnesota.

Raisin Pie

1 c. raisins
1 c. sugar

¼ c. flour
2 tbsp. cold water

2 egg yolks

Cook raisins till tender and add sugar. Stir egg yolks and flour. Thin with cold water and add to raisins. Cook until thick and add 1 tsp. of lemon. Pour in a baked shell and cover with beaten egg whites and brown in oven.—Mrs. J. H. Lewis, South Dakota.

Hawaiian Pineapple Pie

Mix ½ c. each hot water and syrup drained from crushed Hawaiian pineapple or (1 c. juice). Bring to boiling point and add slowly: 3 tbsp. cornstarch and ¾ c. sugar which have been well mixed together. Boil for 3 min., stirring constantly, remove from fire and add: 1 tsp. butter; 3 tbsp. lemon juice; ¾ c. drained crushed pineapple; 2 be..ten egg yolks. Pour into pastry lined pie dish and bake until pastry is well browned. Remove and cool slightly and cover with meringue and brown. —Mrs. Archie Bvobst, Missouri.

Cream Puffs

1 c. flour   ¼ tsp. salt
1 c. boiling water   ½ c. butter
4 eggs

Add the salt and butter to the water. When boiling add the flour all at once, stirring constantly until mixture leaves the side of pan. Remove from fire and add the unbeaten eggs one at a time beating continuously. Drp by spoonsful into slightly greased muffin pans which have been slightly dusted with flour. Bake in a moderate oven for 25 min., when cool cut off top and fill with whipped sweetened and flavored cream.—Mrs. Dan Ewy, Colorado.

French Chocolate Puffs

Bring ½ c. butter and 1 c. hot water to a boil, then quickly stir in 1 c. flour and 2 tbsp. sugar, stirring constantly until the paste clings around the spoon. Remove from the fire, cool, beating a minute for each, then 5 min. after all are in. Set the paste on ice for 1 hr., then put small tbsp. on greased paper laid on an inverted pan, allowing plenty of room to spread. Bake in a moderate oven for 30 min. not opening the door once until time is up. Let cool, then, with the shears, cut a slit in side of each puff and fill with following cream: Put 1½ c. milk in a double boiler, scald and add: 3 tbsp. corn-starch, ¾ c. sugar mixed, stirring constantly. When it begins to thicken beat in 1 tbsp. scrapped chocolate. When nearly cold add ½ tsp. vanilla, put in puffs when cold. Make the icing with 1 c. sugar and 5 tbsp. water. Cook until it forms soft ball in water. Add 2 squares chocolate and stir until melted. When cold add ½ tsp. vanilla. Ice puffs; complete each with tiny rosette of whipped cream or preserve in little egg white and beat stiff, add 1 tbsp. sugar to whites, color pink with currant jelly. Set each little puff in a paper frill.—Mrs. J. W. Haggard, Missouri.

Mock Lemon Pie

2 egg yolks well beaten   1 tsp. butter
Pinch of salt   1 c. boiling water
⅔ c. sugar   1 tbsp. flour (heaping)
3 tbsp. cider vinegar   Mixed with little water
1 tsp. lemon extract

Put everything in water. Add flour paste and cook till it thickens and pour in a baked crust. Cover with stiffly beaten egg whites and brown.—Mrs. Paul Huntly, Colorado.

Ice Cream Pie

Fill individual pie shells with ice cream, cover with crushed pineapple, then a layer of whipped cream and a candied cherry.—Amanda Gunther, Illinois.

Chess Pie

5 eggs	2 c. cream
⅔ c. sugar	½ c. butter
2 tbsp. flour	Vanilla

Mix well. Pour into pie pans lined with unbaked pie crust. Bake in moderate oven.—Mrs. Gertrude Watson, Missouri.

Plum Pie

Pit 1 qt. canned plums, and dice them. Add 1½ c. sugar, 2 tbsp. flour, into which has been added ½ tsp. cinnamon. Line the tins with rich pie dough, and fill the crusts with the above ingredients and bake. When done, let cool, and cover with whipped cream, into which 1 tsp. vanilla and 2 tbsp. sugar have been added.—Adelia Lorenzen, Iowa.

Butter Cream Pie

2 eggs	¾ c. cold milk
½ c. sugar	2 tbsp. butter
3 tbsp. flour	½ tsp. vanilla
1 c. cold water	¼ tsp. peach or almond
Baked pastry shell	

Beat the egg yolks; rub flour and sugar together; add to yolks, add water, milk and butter and cook over hot water until thick, stirring constantly. Cool, add flavoring and pour into cooled pastry shell. Beat egg whites until stiff, add 4 tbsp. sugar, beat in, then add 2 tbsp. more sugar, beat, pour onto pie and brown in oven.—Mrs. Ora M. Kinser, Missouri.

Vinegar Pie

2 egg yolks	1½ c. boiling water
1 c. sugar	3 tbsp. vinegar
2 tbsp. cornstarch	Lemon flavoring

Cook in double boiler till thick and pour into baked crust. Use egg whites for meringue.—Mrs. J. J. Curfman, Iowa.

Custard Pie

First line a deep pie plate with a crust which has been rolled thin, about 2 hr. before you wish to make the pie. Build up a rim around the edges of crust, pinching in little ridges, with your fingers. For the filling heat 1 pt. rich milk to the boiling point. Beat 2 large eggs with ½ c. sugar and a pinch of salt, nutmeg or other flavoring. Add the scalding milk and stir thoroughly. Place your plate in hot oven and fill with the mixture and bake until custard is firm and rich brown. Do not have oven hot enough to boil custard, or it will whey. You may add ½ c. shredded cocoanut and have cocoanut custard. Use 1 tsp. vanilla.—Mrs. I. O. Merrell, Oklahoma.

Cherry Pie

Plain pie pastry for crusts
2 c. cherries
½ c. juice

2 tbsp. min. tapioca or
⅓ c. flour
⅔ to 1 c. sugar

2 tbsp. butter

Line pie pan with crust, sprinkle 1 tbsp. of tapioca over the bottom, add cherries then the rest of tapioca, then the juice and sugar, dot with butter and cover with crust. Bake as other fruit pies. Delicious.—Miss Hattie M. Thomas, Texas.

Rhubarb Pie

Pour boiling water over 2 c. rhubarb; let stand 5 min. and drain. Add 1 c. sugar; a small piece of butter; 1 tbsp. flour, 3 tbsp. water; yolks of 2 eggs. Bake with one crust. Beat whites of eggs stiff with 3 tbsp. sugar. Spread over pie and brown.—Mrs. Fred C. Speckman, Illinois.

Pastry

The secret of good pastry lies in having all ingredients thoroughly chilled. Cut the fat in the flour with 2 silver knives. Use water in proportion of 1:2 to make the dough. Roll in a sheet, fold into 4 layers and roll lightly. Repeat this folding and rolling 4 times. At the last folding do not roll but put on a plate and set out over night or in the ice-box.—Mrs. Arvilla Shain Smith, Illinois.

Pie Crust

Heat the mixing bowl, put 1 c. lard or other cooking fat into the bowl. Add ½ c. boiling water and beat until smooth. Sift 3 c. flour and ½ tsp. baking powder, then stir it into melted fat and water. This may be used at once or kept several days in the ice box. It is to be prepared to use at once.—Miss Maude E. Bernsmeier, Iowa.

Ambrosia Pie

1 can (10 oz.) commercial, moist cocoanut
1½ c. mashed sweet potatoes
3 eggs
½ tsp. nutmeg
2 c. milk (if heated pie will bake faster)
1½ c. sugar
1 tbsp. flour
1 tsp. cinnamon
1 c. whipping cream (for meringue)

Sift dry ingredients together and add to the beaten eggs, milk, and sweet potato. Next put in the cocoanut. Pour into rich pastry shell and bake in a moderate oven (350 degrees) for about 45 min. When pie is cool cover with whipped cream and serve. If a large deep pie is not desired this recipe will make 2 small shallow pies.—Kathryn G. Woodside, New Mex.

Apple Pie

2 c. apples, (sliced)   ¼ c. cream, sweet
     Grimes Golden pre-   1 tsp. cinnamon
     ferred)   2 tbsp. flour
         1 c. brown sugar
Rich pastry: ½ tsp. salt
1 c. flour   Cold water
⅓ c. lard

Fill rich pastry shell with sliced apples, balance of flour, sugar and cinnamon, mixed together over the top. Cover with upper crust, bake in moderate oven. If preferred the pie may be enriched with dots of whipped cream when served.—Mrs. Ira Bishop, Kansas.

Orange Pie

Juice of ½ lemon   1 c. sugar
Juice of 2 oranges   ¼ tsp. salt
Grated rind of 1 orange   3 egg yolks
3 tbsp. butter   1 egg white
1 tbsp. flour   1 tbsp. cold water

Beat the eggs, and add sugar, butter and flour and salt. Then add orange and lemon juice and grated rind, and water. Mix well and bake in one crust until done. Cover top of pie with two egg whites, well beaten.—Mrs. Otis E. Young, Oklahoma.

Pumpkin Pies

1¾ c. sugar   1 tsp. ginger
2 tbsp. flour   1 tsp. cinnamon
1 tsp. salt   ½ tsp. allspice
         ¼ tsp. cloves

Mix all above together and add 2 c. cooked pumpkin or ½ can pumpkin. Add yolks of 3 eggs. Mix thoroughly and add the beaten white of eggs. Also add 2 c. rich milk. Bake slowly until thoroughly set and browned. Makes 2 large pies. The stiffly beaten whites make them puffy and form a sort of meringue.—Mrs. A. L. Dick, Kansas.

Graham Cracker Pie

1 c. graham cracker crumbs   ½ c. sugar
6 tbsp. butter   3 tbsp. cornstarch
1 c. milk   2 eggs

Melt butter and pour over cracker crumbs. Mix so that it holds together. Line pie tin with this. Boil milk, cornstarch, sugar yolks, of eggs, till thick. If needed, one may add a little more cornstarch. Pour into pan. Beat whites of eggs very stiff. Top the pie with this and sprinkle with cracker crumbs and brown.—Miss Bernice Klozinak, Wisconsin.

CHEESE

Baked Macaroni With Cheese

1 c. macaroni
1 tbsp. flour
1 tbsp. butter
1 c. milk

½ c. grated cheese
1 tsp. paprika
1 tsp. salt
⅛ tsp. pepper

Boil macaroni in salted water until soft; drain and rinse with cold water. Put into buttered baking dish and cover with sauce. Cover top with grated cheese and bake 20 min. in hot oven. Sauce for this: Melt butter in saucepan; add flour, mix well and add cold milk slowly, stirring until smooth; add cheese, salt, pepper and paprika.—Mary Schneider, Kansas.

Macaroni and Cheese

¾ c. macaroni
½ c. grated cheese

1½ qt. boiling water
1½ c. white sauce

1 tbsp. salt

Drop macaroni in boiling salted water, cook until soft, drain, put in buttered baking dish, cover with white sauce in which the cheese has been melted. Sprnkle with bread crumbs, bake until brown. White Sauce: 2 tbsp. butter; ½ tsp. salt; 2 tbsp. flour; 1 c. canned milk. Melt butter until it stops bubbling, stir in flour and mix thoroughly, add milk, stirring until thick and smooth, and season.—Mrs. Joe San Sebastain, California.

Real Italian Spaghetti

4 slices bacon (cut small)
1 small onion (diced)
1 pkg long spaghetti

1 can tomatoes (large)
1 c. cheese (diced)
Seasoning

Brown quickly bacon and onion in heavy iron skillet. Remove from grease and thoroughly brown 1 package spaghetti broken small. Add bacon, onion and can of tomatoes. If tomatoes aren't real juicy add hot water. Season well with salt, pepper and parika. Allow to simmer for ¾ hr. Add 1 c. diced cheese and cook enough to allow cheese to melt.—Camilla J. Derby, Nebraska.

Welsh Rarebit

1½ c. cheese (diced)
2 eggs
2 tbsp. flour
½ tsp. salt
⅛ tsp. mustard

Few grains of paprika
2 tbsp. butter (omit if desired
⅛ tsp. pepper

Mix ingredients in the order given in a double boiler top. Add milk and stir over hot water until thick and smooth. Serve on toast or crisp crackers.—Mrs. Florence Watts, Kansas.

Cheese Roast

1 can peas or kidney beans (drained)
6 hard boiled eggs chopped
½ lb. cheese
1 onion
1 c. bread crumbs
1 tbsp. butter

Salt and pepper to taste. Put peas and cheese through meat chopper. Cook onion with butter and a little water. Put all together. Make into a loaf and bake 30 min. Serve with tomato sauce.—Mrs. Hans Skoar, North Dakota.

Cheese Souffle

2 tbsp. flour
2 tbsp. butter
3 eggs
1 c. cheese
Salt and pepper
½ c. hot milk

Melt butter, add flour, add milk, cook until thick and add cheese, remove from fire, beat egg yolks, add to mixture. Salt and pepper to taste. Return to fire until eggs are cooked. Fold in stiffly beaten whites. Bake in moderate oven 20 min. Serve immediately.—Mrs. L. L. Sheink, Kansas.

Cheese Pudding

1 c. scalded milk
1 c. soft bread crumbs
¼ lb. cheese
½ tsp. salt
1 tbsp. butter
3 eggs beaten separately

Mix all together, then add egg yolks. Fold in egg whites carefully. Bake 20 min. in buttered baking dish.—Beulah Hauser, Iowa.

Pink Poodle

1½ tbsp. butter
1½ c. strained tomato juice
2½ tbsp. flour
1½ c. milk
1½ c. grated cheese
2 eggs
Salt
Cayenne

Melt butter, add flour slowly, add milk and tomato juice. Then egg well beaten. Lastly add cheese and when melted add seasoning. Delicious served hot on crisp toast or crackers.— Pauline R. Hayen, Kansas.

Cheese

I take an old 3 gal. enamel bucket and punch holes in the bottom and sides half way up the sides which I use for the press. I take 1 gal. of whole milk that is sweet put in the boiler and heat to (98 degrees F.) I have ready 1½ Rennet Tablets dissolved in ½ glass lukewarm water and 1 cheese coloring tablet, thoroughly dissolved in ½ glass of lukewarm water. Set the milk off stove and add coloring and the rennet and stir 3 min. Lay bread board over boiler and some padding of some kind over that to keep it warm for 30 min. Then it will be set like clabber milk. Run a knife clear through and mark into squares. Let set a few min. then dip into a thin clean flour sack. Let the sack set in a colander over the boiler, moving every few min. until it drains out the water, then put in a pan, mix salt to taste, then put back in sack. It's better to make a sack the shape of a bucket and put the whole in your bucket and cover with a plate and put a big rock on top and set it where it can drain for 24 hrs. Remove from the press and sack and spread warm butter over all, put on a platter, cover with a thin cloth and turn it over every day. In 2 weeks, it is sure good. Don't allow to freeze but keep in a moderately warm place to cure.—Mrs. Della Wright, Missouri.

Cream Cheese

1 gal sweet milk
1 qt. sour milk, not buttermilk
6 eggs
1 c. sour cream

Heat the sweet milk to boiling, have the sour milk and cream ready with beaten eggs in it. Stir the mixture into boiling milk and let cook for 5 min. Then take it away to cool and have cheese cloth ready and some kind of a mold, wooden one preferred. Put some of the curd into the mold and about 1 tsp. fine salt, sprinkled in. Do this alternately till it is all in. Let cool and drain for 6-7 hrs. and then turn on a plate and it is ready to eat.—Mrs. Waino Pentrila, Washington.

Creamy Eggs With Cottage Cheese

1 c. milk
1 tbsp. flour
4 eggs
1 c. cottage cheese
¼ tsp. soda
1 tbsp. fat
½ tsp. pepper
½ tsp. salt
Paprika
Parsley or pimentos

Make a thick sauce with the milk, flour, fat and seasoning. Cook five min. and pour gradually on the cheese, which has been neutralized with the soda dissolved in a little of the milk. When the cheese and sauce are well blended, return them to the top of the double boiler and reheat over hot water. Beat the eggs, pour them into the warm sauce and mix well. The mixture is cooked when it is of a creamy consistency throughout. This serves 10 persons.—Marie Britton, Wisconsin.

Scalloped Eggs With Cheese

6 hard boiled eggs
2 c. white sauce
2 c. buttered soft bread
crumbs
¾ c. cheese
White sauce is made with:
¾ tbsp. fat
1 tbsp. flour
1 c. milk (twice each for
2 c.)

Grate cheese and add to white sauce and cut eggs in slices. Oil a baking dish and place in layers, have lower and top layers bread crumbs. Bake in moderate oven until light and the mixture is heated through and crumbs are browned. Serve hot in place of meat.—Mrs. Chas. Talley, Arkansas.

Spanish Cheese

1 tbsp. minced red pepper or dash of cayenne
1 c. tomato pulp or tomato soup
2 eggs   1 tbsp. grated onion
1 lb. American cheese   1½ c. milk
1 tbsp. butter

Melt the butter in a sauce pan and add the onions and red pepper and seasoning. Cook for few min., then add the tomato pulp. Mix well and when bubbling stir in the cheese, cut in small pieces. Cook over slow fire, stirring constantly. Beat eggs and add milk and then add to mixture. Cook 2 min. Serve at once on toast or crisp waffles.—Mrs. Flora Helbert, Indiana.

Farm Cheese

2 gallons clabber milk. Heat and strain out the curd as in making cottage cheese. To the curd add:

2 egg yolks   1 level tsp. soda
Butter size of walnut   1 tsp salt

Put in double boiler and stir until curd melts into a smooth batter. Pour in dish to mold, when cold slice, will look and taste like cream cheese.—Lillie McFerran, Ind.

Plain Omelets

1 tbsp butter   3 tbsp. milk
4 eggs   ½ tsp. salt
Speck of pepper

Melt the butter in baking pan, being careful that butter does not burn. Separate eggs. Beat the yolks with water and seasoning. Beat the whites until dry and fold into the yolks. Pour the mixture into the buttered pan and cook very slowly on stove 5 min. Then finish cooking in slow oven. Fold when ready to serve—turning it on a hot platter. Serve with white sauce if desired—at once.—Mrs. Chas. Oakes, N. Dak.

Egg A la Swisse

4 eggs   1 tbsp. butter
½ c. crea m   2 tbsp. grated cheese
Salt, pepper, cayenne

Heat a small omelet pan, put in butter and when melted add cream. Slip the eggs 1 at a time. Sprinkle with salt and a few grains of cayenne. When whites are nearly firm sprinkle with cheese. Finish cooking and serve on buttered toast. Strain the cream over the toast.—Mrs. Henry J. Untiedt, Minn.

Stuffed Eggs

½ doz. eggs
1 tsp. butter
2 tbsp. salad dressing

3 small sweet pickles
(chopped fine)
⅛ tsp. celery seed

Boil eggs 4 min. cut in halves lengthwise. Remove yolks and add to them butter salad dressing, salt then pepper and celery seed, Mix thoroughly then add pickles. Stir the mixture well and leave in halves or fasten together with toothpicks which ever you desire.—Mrs. Harry Goodwin, Ind.

Hot Deviled Eggs

Prepare as for ordinary deviled eggs and after skewering the two halves together with toothpicks, roll them in egg and then in fine dry bread or cracker crumbs. Then dip them in beaten egg and into the crumbs again, and fry them in deep fat till golden brown. Remove toothpicks and serve hot, with Epicurean sauce, made as follows:

3 tbsp mayonnaise
1 tbsp prepared mustard

3 tbsp. grated horseradish
½ c. whipped cream

1 tsp. Worcestershire sauce

Mix in order given.—Mrs. Cris Spiker, Ia.

Eggs A'La Goldenrod

3 hard boiled eggs
1 tbsp butter
1 tbsp flour

1 c. sweet milk
½ tsp. salt
⅛ tsp. pepper

5 slices toast

Make a thin white sauce with butter, milk, flour and seasonings. Separate yolks from whites of eggs. Chop whites finely and add them to the sauce. Cut 4 slices of toast in ½ lengthwise and arrange on platter and pour the sauce over. Force the yolks thru the potato ricer or strainer, sprinkle over the top. Garnish with the remaining pieces of toast cut in points. —Miss Martha Roberts, Ind.

MEAT

Ravioli

1 lb. juicy steak (cut in cubes)
Saute this in plenty of drippings

Add 1 onion cut fine
3 or 4 pimentoes chopped
1 small bottle olives
2 bay leaves and few cloves

Salt, pepper, cayenne, paprika to suit taste

After frying meat, add hot water and let simmer until done. Add 1 can mushrooms and a little olive oil. Have a pan of tender boiled spaghetti. Pour this spaghetti on platter and cover with the meat. Pour over top of this cream cheese grated. Serve on toast or with hot rolls.—Mrs. Norman LeCompte, Mo.

Flank Steak en Casserole

1 flank steak
1 tbsp lemon juice
1½ tsp. salt
1 tbsp. onion, minced

Speck pepper, nutmeg and cloves
1 c. crumbs
1 c. tomatoes

1 pt. hot water or tomato stock

Score the steak closely on both sides and rub the seasonings over one side of the steak. Roll, tie with a string, and sear. Place in a deep frying pan. Pour in water or stock. Cover and bake in a moderate oven or simmer until tender. Thicken the stock and serve around the steak. Time in oven, 2 hr. Temperature (350°). Serves 8.—Mrs. Chas. Oakes, N. Dak.

Baked Ham

Soak ham over night, then wash and scrape it. Put in in cold water, let it come to boiling point, then simmer for 2 hr. Let ham cool in the water, then remove and draw off skin. Bake in moderate oven for 2 hr., baste frequently, using 1 c. peach juice (left over from canned or pickled peaches), 2 tbsp. of butter. When done cover with a paste of prepared mustard, flour and brown sugar moistened with peach juice and return to oven and brown. —Mrs. Joe Maher, Ia.

Pot Roast of Beef with Dumplings

4 lbs. top sirloin of beef
1 qt. water
1 c. canned tomatoes
Seasoning

Onions, carrots and turnips
3 tbsp. drippings or other fat

Have the meat cut in a thick, compact piece. If necessary, tie and skewer so it will keep its shape. Melt a little fat in a saucepan and brown the meat on all sides; pour the boiling water over, add the tomatoes and cover closely. Simmer as gently as possible for 2 hr. Season, and add vegetables scraped or peeled as they need, and cut into pieces. Cook till the vegetables are tender then remove the meat and vegetables and add the dumplings. If necessary add more water while roast is cooking that there may be sufficient gravy to cover vegetables. Dumplings: 1½ c. flour; ½ tsp. salt; 1½ tsp. baking powder sifted with flour; milk to mix a soft dough that will drop from a spoon. Drop in the pan, cover closely and do not remove cover until they are done. Cook about 20 min.—Mrs. A. L. Rockwell, Mo.

Pork Chops en Casserole

6 pork chops
6 sweet potatoes

Salt and pepper
½ c. brown sugar

1 or 2 c. milk

Place a layer of sweet potatoes sliced crosswise in a greased casserole until the casserole is about ⅔ full. Heat the milk and pour it over the potatoes; it should just cover them. Place the pork chops on top of the potatoes, cover and bake for 1 hr., then remove the cover and season with salt and pepper. Leave the cover off and cook until the chops are tender, and nicely browned on the top. The brown sugar is sprinkled over the sweet potatoes before the milk is poured over them.—Mrs. W. R. Curry, Ark.

Fried Bananas and Bacon

Fry bacon until crisp, allowing two slices to each person. Into the hot bacon drippings drop bananas sliced lengthwise, fry to a golden brown; sprinkle with powdered sugar and serve on toast between slices of bacon.—Miss Leona Petersen, Nebr.

Young Roast Pig

Select a pig not over 6 or 8 weeks old. Have it neatly dressed leaving the head, feet and tail intact. Rub the inside of the pig with salt and pepper and lay thin slices of salt pork along the backbone. Fill with dressing as for turkey then sew firmly together with a cord. Put in a large baking pan with the knees turned under, and a small cob in its mouth to keep it open. Put a little water in a pan and after 20 min. commence to baste and continue at regular intervals, until it is brown and tender. Place on a platter on its knees. Serve with apple sauce.—Mrs. Albie Horn, Wyo.

Spare Ribs With Apples

1 side of pork ribs   6 apples

Salt

Split the ribs down through the center. Place ½ the side in a covered roaster, and salt. On top of this put a row of cored apples, placing the other half of the ribs, salted on top of the apples. Cover the roaster and bake slowly 1½ to 2 hrs.— Lucile Ingram, Texas.

Ham Baked in Raisin Sauce

Boil a slice of ham 1½ in. thick in 1 qt. water in which ⅓ c. brown sugar has been added. When almost done pour off water and place in a roaster with 1 c. raisins, 1 tbsp. brown sugar and 1 c. water. Bake till dark brown and add more water if needed and thicken gravy with flour.—Mrs. Warren Printy, Md.

Lamb Chops

6 lamb shoulder chops   1 c. thick white sauce
1 tsp. horseradish   ¼ c. grated cheese
1 tbsp. butter   ¼ c. bread crumbs

Melt the butter, add horseradish and white sauce. Spread each chop with the sauce. Grate cheese over the top with a sprinkle of bread crumbs. Put in a pan and cook in a hot oven (400°) until tender and brown about 45 min. Serves 6.—Mrs. Edith DeBarry, Ark.

Use of Mutton and Lamb on Ranch

When we dress a mutton for home use the hind quarters are roasted and canned in a pressure cooker for summer use, the change of beef and pork and chicken canned is of real importance in the country. The front quarters make nice roast. The ribs are stewed just below the chops, in small pieces boiled with the addition of onion, carrot for seasoning, boiled down for just enough gravy, thickened and dumplings made and steamed just before dinner, the neck and coarse parts are boiled, ground in food chopper and seasoned with salt, pepper, and a little nutmeg, some of it is used as pressed meat with gelatine, some for a hash, some in meat pie or fried as meat balls. Lamb is cut in convenient pieces for frying, a saddle is stuffed with any favorite filling and roasted. The hind leg of lamb is fine dipped in a batter like pancake batter a little stiffer. Placed in covered roaster and roasted slowly till tender. It will be real juicy and more tender than not covered with batter. The liver of both lamb and mutton are used and are nice sliced, fried or baked whole, or sliced and a slice of bacon rolled in each slice and fried. A nice liver pudding is made by boiling liver gently till blood sets, ground and a little boiled bacon cut in minced squares seasoned with nutmeg, pepper, salt and mashed potatoes. Bake in oven for about ½ hr. Set to cool, and slice.—Mrs. G. W. Wolff, S. Dak.

Irish Stew

1 lb. lamb from fore quarter or of beef stew meat, such as shoulder or rump. Wipe and cut 1½ in. pieces. Dredge with flour and brown in hot fat in a kettle. Cover with boiling water and cook 2 or 3 hr. or until tender. 1 hr. before meat is done, add ¼ c. each of diced carrots, turnips, and onions. ½ hr. later, add 1½ c. diced potatoes. If desired the meat and vegetables may be removed, the gravy thickened and the meat and vegetables again returned to the kettle.—Mrs. Elizabeth Sharp, Nebr.

Beef Meat Loaf

2 lb. beef and 1 lb. pork (ground)	1 tsp. salt
1 medium sized onion	1 pepper
2 eggs beaten	½ c. bread crumbs
	1 can tomato soup

Make a loaf and roll in crumbs and pour over balance of tomato soup and little water. Bake 2 hr. slowly.—Mrs. Wm. Selfors, N. Dak.

Dutch Roast

3 lbs. round steak 1½ in. thick	6 small Irish potatoes
	1 medium onion

Salt and pepper

Dredge the steak well on both sides with flour. Place in skillet with bottom covered with hot shortening. Brown on both sides. Cover with hot water. Cover and cook until nearly tender. Pare the potatoes and place in skillet and around the steak. Slice onion and place on top. Cover and cook until all are done. More water may be added if necessary. You have your potatoes, meat and rich gravy all cooked in one dish. Serve the steak on a platter with potatoes around it. The gravy serve separately.—Mrs. Chas. L. Starkey, Texas.

Spanish Steak

2 lbs. round steak	1 pt. canned tomatoes
½ bay leaf	6 whole cloves
1 onion	6 peppercorns

Few gratings of lemon rind

Dredge steak in flour, sear in hot fat in which onion has been browned. Season with salt and pepper. Place in baking dish and cover with strained tomatoes and seasonings and cook

with a cover in slow oven for 2 hr. or until meat is tender.—
Mrs. Elizabeth Sharp, Nebr.

Veal Cutlets, with Cream Gravy

Have the cutlets or kidney chops, cut ¾ in. thick. Roll these
in well seasoned flour and cook in frying pan. Use ¼ c. butter
or bacon fat but salt pork is best. When well browned add
½ c. boiling water. Place quarters of green bell peppers on top
of meat. Cover close and reduce heat. Let simmer 20 min.
remove meat and peppers to hot platter and make the gravy.
To 3 tbsp. of fat, in pan add 3 tbsp. of flour and stir well and
pour in 1½ c. milk. Cook slowly and stir constantly until
smooth and thickened. Season as desired and strain around
the meat. Minced onion may be added to the fat in making
the gravy if liked.—Marie Jess, Kan.

Baked Breaded Veal

Dip slices of veal steak in beaten egg and bread crumbs. Fry
quickly in butter or fresh bacon grease until brown. Salt and
pepper to taste. Pile the slices of fried meat in a baking dish,
on top of each other. Make generous quantity of gravy and
pour over the meat, covering well. Bake very slowly for 2 or
3 hr. in covered dish. When done the meat will be very tender
and the gravy cooked low. If more gravy is desired, it can be
made after taking meat out of baking dish.—Mrs. Geo. E.
Rossman, Ill.

Veal Birds

1½ lbs. veal	2 c. milk
2 c. bread crumbs	1½ tsp. salt
1 tbsp. onion (cut fine)	2 or 3 bay leaves
1 egg	Cut veal in slices 3 by 5 in.

Make a dressing of crumbs, onion and bay leaf, salt and egg.
Spread each slice of veal with dressing nearly to the edge. Roll
tightly and fasten with a slice of bacon around each roll, with
a toothpick. Dredge birds in flour, pepper and salt and brown
in hot fat. Add a little water and let steam until tender.—Miss
Flora Girch, Nebr.

Washday Dinner

Use a large, flat pan, enamel or aluminum. Melt 1 tbsp. of
butter in it. Slice a thick layer of onions, then a generous
layer of Irish potatoes. Sift 2 tbsp. of flour over this. Pour
a can of tomatoes, (use large can if for large family), slice
sausages thinly and cover the top. Cover with boiling water
salted to taste, and bake slowly three hrs. If sausages get too
brown turn them over. This is a Greek recipe, and is so tasty
that it will not be confined to washday if once tried.—Mrs.
John Franke, Texas.

Meat Balls

2 tbsp. rice (uncooked)	1 lb. hamburger
1 egg	¼ lb. pork

Salt and pepper

Stir all together and make into balls. Drop into liquid made as follows:

1 can tomatoes	1 small onion (chopped)
1 tsp. chili pepper	Salt and pepper

Cook slowly for 1½ hr. either in moderate oven, or a slow fire. Delicious.—Mrs. Virgil Ferguson, Indiana.

Baked Corn Beef Hash

3 c. chopped cooked corned beef	2 tbsp. bacon fat
	1½ c. milk
6 good sized potatoes	Salt and pepper to taste
1 onion	1 tbsp. chopped pepper

Put chopped corned beef in casserole or roaster, well greased and add onion chopped pepper and put sliced potatoes on top. Arrange in layers and season throughout. Pour milk over all and cover and bake until potatoes are tender, then brown 10 min. with cover off.—Mrs. W. B. Little, Illinois.

Stuffed Calves Heart

Wash the hearts, remove veins, arteries and clotted blood. Make a bread dressing highly seasoned with sage, and stuff and sew. Sprinkle with salt and pepper and roll in flour and brown in hot fat. Place in small deep baking pan, half cover them with boiling water, cover closely and bake slowly 2 hrs. If necessary, add more water. Remove hearts from pan and thicken the liquid with flour made smooth with cold water. Season with salt and pepper. Pour around hearts before serving.—Mrs. W. L. Paul, Missouri.

Pigs in Blankets

Make a rich biscuit dough. Roll as thin as a nickle. Lay frankfurters on dough and roll until edges meet. Cut right across and pinch at ends. Place on a biscuit pan and bake until a golden brown. Split open and add mustard. Serve immediately.—Grace Whitmarsh, Pennsylvania.

Chop Suey

1 lb round steak	3 large green peppers
1 stalk celery	3 or 4 onions

1 can tomatoes

Cut steak into small pieces and fry brown in butter, cut celery, onion and peppers and add with tomatoes to meat and cook well done. Serve with rich or mashed potatoes.—Mrs. Rose Fish, Illinois.

Liver Postie

3 lb. liver	2 tbsp. flour
1 lb. fat	1 c. bread crumbs
1½ lb. med. lean pork	6 eggs
2 good sized onions	1 pt. cream

1 pt. soup or milk and cream

Pepper, cloves and allspice and salt to taste. Mix all thoroughly. Put liver, fat, and lean pork and onions through the food chopper twice. Bake in medium hot oven till done.—Mrs. Albert Aspelin, Kansas.

Baked Liver Delicious

1½ lbs. beef liver	½ c. water
1 c. cream or milk	3 tbsp. butter
2 apples, sliced	3 slices bacon
½ c. raisins	1½ tsp. salt

⅛ tsp. pepper

Flour to dredge. Use a thick piece of liver, soak several hours or over night in sour milk or buttermilk, cut liver on the thick side to make a pocket, and in this place the apples, raisins, the butter arranged in dots and some of the salt. Sew the liver together, make cuts on top surface of the liver and fill the cavities this makes, with pieces of bacon held in place by toothpicks. Dredge the cavities with flour before adding the bacon. Place in a baking dish and add the water. Bake in a moderate oven about 2 hrs., baste frequently. When cooked place the liver on a platter, thicken the drippings in the pan, add the cream or milk and the seasonings and serve with the meat.—Miss Estelle Sanders, Alabama.

Fricassee Rabbit

Clean 2 young rabbits and cut into joints and soak in salt water for 1 hr. Put in a sauce pan: Add 1 pt. cold water, onion finely chopped, pinch of mace, pinch of pepper, ½ lb. salt pork cut into slices; cover and stew until tender. Take out rabbit. Add to the gravy: 2 tsp. flour, 1 c. cream. Boil till thick and pour over the rabbit and serve hot.—Mrs. Cora Cumbie, Arkansas.

Pickled Pigs Feet

Clean feet and boil tender in water, with ⅔ c. vinegar, 1 tsp. mixed spice and 1 tbsp. salt. When done, take out and cool liquid, remove, fat and reheat liquid, and pour over the feet. Good when cold.—Mrs. F. W. Krause, South Dakota.

Pork Chops with Tomato Gravy

Rub the chops over with sage and onion. Put small piece of butter into frying pan. Put in the chops and cook slowly as they should be well done. Lay chops on hot dish; add a little hot water to gravy in pan, 1 large spoon of butter, rolled in flour, pepper, salt and a little sugar and ½ c. tomato juice. Stew 5 min. and pour over chops and serve.—Mrs. Ray Douglas, Kansas.

Pork Chops with Dressing

8 chops
½ tsp. salt
½ tsp. chopped onion
1 tbsp. melted butter
1 egg yolk

1½ c. bread crumbs
¼ tsp. celery seed
Little chopped parsley or green pepper
1 tbsp. of water

Mix the dressing, wipe the chops and place one in small pan. Spread the dressing on it and press the other chop on top. Bake in a moderate oven 1 hr., basting with hot water in which some butter has been added. Turn to brown the under chop. Place 1 tbsp. water in bottom of pan to prevent burning and replenish when necessary.—Mrs. Dora Wade, Kansas.

Shepard's Pie

1½ lbs. ground beef or mutton
Season to taste

1 egg
4 c. mashed potatoes
1 med. sized onion cut fine

Place meat with an onion, egg and seasoning in a dripping pan or casserole. Set in oven until juice begins to form. Have your mashed potatoes ready and put on top of the meat with pieces of butter dotting the top. Bake until potatoes are beginning to brown. Sometimes I put a can of small peas between the meat and potatoes.—Mrs. Wm. Weiser, New York.

Post Toasties Dressing

4 c. post toasties
4 pieces light brown toast
2 pieces cornbread about 2 in. square

8 or 10 crackers
1 can cove oysters or the giblets cut up fine
———

Season with salt and pepper with a taste of sage or onion if desired. Onion may be omitted. Moisten this with enough cooled broth of chicken or turkey so it can be handled with the hands to mold. Set in oven to brown. This makes stuffing also. —Mrs. M. J. Dare, Wyoming.

POULTRY AND GAME

Chicken a la King

3 c. cooked chicken	3 tbsp. butter
1 c. chicken stock or broth	¼ lb. mushrooms or ½ can
1 c. thin cream or	½ green pepper shredded
(1 c. evaporated milk)	1 tsp. salt
3 tbsp. flour	¼ tsp. paprika
3 tbsp. chicken fat	2 egg yolks

Cut the chicken in cubes before measuring. Add green pepper, salt, paprika and a dash of nutmeg. Cooked the sliced mushrooms in the butter very slowly for 10 min. Melt the chicken fat, add the flour, and stir until smooth. Add gradu-

JULINE.

ally the cream, stir to a smooth sauce. Add chicken mixture and mushrooms; let boil up, then pull back and add beaten egg yolks. Do not let boil after this, as that will curdle the eggs. Keep hot over hot water. Serve on toast; parsey garnish. Serves 8. ½ c. sifted peas may be added if desired to make 10 servings.—Mrs. Geo. E. Rossman, Ill.

Chicken Pie

Cook chicken till nearly tender, salt and finish cooking. Remove bones. Place meat in baking dish and add sauce made as follows: 3 tbsp. flour, 5 c. chicken broth, 1 c. cream. Pour over the chicken and place in oven and heat through. Cover with batter made as follows: Sift together 2 c. flour, ½ tsp. salt and 2 heaping tsp. baking powder. Work 2 tsp. butter into the flour and add 1 well beaten egg and 1 c. sweet milk. Beat till smooth, pour over chicken and bake 30 min.—Mrs. Flora Helbert, Ind.

Pressed Chicken

Stew chicken slowly until meat drops from bone. Take out and put through food chopper and let the broth boil down to 1 c. Add to it butter the size of an egg, ½ tsp. black pepper and salt to taste, and 1 egg. Remove broth from fire while adding egg to prevent curdling. Stir well and boil 1 or 2 min. Then add meat. Have a mold ready to cover bottom with sliced boiled eggs, placing a few slices around the sides of mold as the meat is pressed in. When cold slice and serve plain or with dressing.—Mrs. Otis E. Young, Okla.

Fricassee of Chicken

Jointed fat hen	2 c. tomatoes strained thru
Salt and roll in flour	sieve
4 tbsp. fat	1 c. water and pepper to
1 tbsp. chilli powder	taste
1 small minced onion	¼ tsp. rosemary leaves
⅛ tsp. powdered thyme	

Use a steamer if possible or any roaster with a tight cover. Put in the roaster when hot, the fat, chili powder and the onion, then brown the chicken which has been rolled in flour and salted. Put in other ingredients. Cover tight, put on back of stove or in oven and cook slowly about 2 hr. When ready to serve have ready 1 c. water; 1 tbsp. flour; mix together, stir into the gravy and add salt to taste.—Ethel Carpenter, Kan.

Chicken Dressing

Use ½ loaf dry hard bread. Soak in cold water until it is thoroly moist and falls apart. Add 3 beaten eggs, salt and pepper to suit taste and 1 tsp. powdered sage. Then add 3 small onions, 4 apples and the heart, liver and gizzard of fowl which have been put through the food chopper. Mix with milk or water enough to make a medium thick mixture. Stuff the fowl and what is left place in roaster around fowl or in separate pan if clear gravy is desired.—Mrs. James Jaenicke, Kan.

Baked Goose

Remove all the larger feathers dry, then cover the fowl with melted parafin, and allow to cool. All the down, and small feathers will come off with the parafin. Put an onion inside the goose and cook until tender, salting as desired. Remove the onion and squeeze lemon juice over the outside of the goose, and brown in oven, with or without dressing.—Mrs. F. H. Boone, Okla.

Roast Guinea

There is no better table fowl than young guineas. They have a flavor similar to prairie chickens or quails. Being grain eaters and are very clean in their habits they are quite similar to turkeys but have almost no white meat. Dress as you would any fowl, cool over night, season with salt and pepper, pack with your favorite dressing. Strips of bacon laid across the breast and drum sticks are a help but not essential. Three young guineas if small or 2 large will serve six people very well. Serve with them just what you would with a turkey.—N. Maud Bever, Nebr.

Roast Turkey

When turkey is dressed, rub inside with salt and hang up to dry for 1 hr. Wipe dry with a cloth, put dressing in and sew up. Tie legs together to the body. When ready for the oven, melt a little lard and spread it on a clean white cloth and lay over turkey. Grease a heavy wrapping paper the same way and lay over cloth and then a still heavier brown paper and lay over all. Put a cup of water in the pan and this will baste the turkey better than the old way. If paper should scorch, replace with a fresh piece. When you want the turkey to brown remove the cloth and papers and brown it. This is extra fine.—Mrs. Oscar Carlson, N. Dak.

Smothered Capon

Dress and joint as usual. Fry in butter or meat drippings, turning until seared on all sides and nice and brown, transfer it to a casserole, and 2 sliced onions, 2 stalks of celery and a small bay leaf. Pour over it 2 c. tomato liquor strained from canned tomatoes, 1 tsp. salt and pepper; cover the casserole closely and put in a steady oven. Cook for 3 hr. looking at it occasionally and filling it up with water to equal the original liquid. When the capon is tender, take it out and keep hot while you thicken the gravy in the casserole with a heaping tbsp. of flour and ½ tbsp. butter.—Mrs. W. A. Parsons, Kan.

FISH

Codfish Surprise

1 lb. dried boned codfish
½ lb. cured bacon sliced thin and delicately browned
10 medium potatoes boiled and mashed.
1 qt. yellow sauce made from the following ingredients:

1 qt. milk	¼ c. butter
½ c. flour	3 egg yolks

Make white sauce of flour, butter and milk, beat egg yolks slightly and add to white sauce. Cook 1 min. add drained codfish. Pile the mashed potatoes on a large platter leaving a hole in center into which the codfish sauce is poured. Whip the whites of eggs and pile on top. Place in oven and brown slightly. Use the piece of crisp bacon as a garnish. (The codfish should be soaked in cold water for 2 hrs. then cut in small pieces and simmer in a small amount of water for 15 min. and drain before adding to the yellow sauce). Delicious. — Ruth C. Kellogg, Iowa.

Salmon Patties

1 can salmon	4 tbsp. cold water
4 eggs	Sifted bread crumbs
2 tbsp. thick cream	2 c. white sauce
½ tsp. salt	½ c. finely cut celery
Pinch of pepper	8 slices of toast

Flake the salmon, add 2 eggs, slightly beaten, the cream salt and pepper. Mix and shape in small flat cakes. Coat with 2 eggs beaten with cold water, cover with sifted bread crumbs and saute in butter until well browned on both side. Serve each cake on a slice of hot toast and cover with white sauce to which celery has been added.—Belle Morrison, Missouri.

Baked Salmon

1 can salmon	1 c. cream
1 egg	8 crackers

Salt and pepper

Roll crackers and mix the ingredients thoroughly. Bake in a greased baking dish until brown and serve hot.—Edna Karnes, Ohio.

Baked Halibut and Tomato Sauce

For 2 lb. Halibut	Cook 20 min.
2 c. tomatoes	Add: 3 tbsp melted butter
1 c. water	3 tbsp. flour, stir into hot
1 sliced onion	mixture
3 cloves	⅜ tsp. salt
½ tsp. sugar	⅛ tsp. pepper

Clean the fish and place in baking pan and pour ½ the sauce around it and bake 35 min. Bast often. Remove to hot platter and add remaining sauce and garnish with parsley.—Mrs. Jas. Grody, Illinois.

Shrimp Wiggle

2 cans of Shrimp	1 c. tomatoes
1 c. rice cooked	1 tbsp. chopped onions

1 pt. cream (milk and butter may be used instead)

Butter size of egg. Cook onion in butter. Add tomatoes, and cooked rice. When hot add shrimp, cut in thirds. Add cream, and season with salt and pepper.—Mrs. Louis Reinmuth, Minnesota.

Frog Legs

The green marsh frogs furnish the best hams, as they are more tender and have less of the strong muddy flavor. They are generally liked fried. Pare off the feet and truss them by inserting the stump along the shin of the other leg. Put them with salt, pepper and lemon juice to seep for 1 hr. Then drain and roll in flour, then in beaten egg and in fine bread crumbs. Fry to a light brown in hot fat. Serve with fried parsley.—Miss Nell Redinger, Nebraska.

Toasted Sardines

Take each sardine and lay on an oblong or cracker. Then place the cracker in oven and allow to remain until brown. Nice to serve for luncheon with thin slices of lemon and parsley.—Mary Behrman, Montana.

SOUP

Mock Oyster Soup

The average American family demand soup and good soup. Here is a recipe we often use and it is very good.

12 stalks vegetable oysters   1 tbsp. butter
1 qt. boiling water   Salt and pepper to taste
1 pt. rich milk   Sprig of parsley improves
1 onion (very small)   flavor
1 tbsp. flour

Scrape the vegetable oysters and put them into cold water to which 1 tbsp. of vinegar has been added. This prevents discoloration. Cut into thin slices; put into pan of boiling water with onion and sprig of parsley. Cook slowly 30 min. Put milk into double boiler, add butter and flour rubbed together and stir until it is smooth and begins to thicken. Add the cooked vegetable and serve at once.—Mrs. Fern Berry, Michigan.

Baby's Vegetable Soup

1 c. carrots   1 tsp. salt
Handful spinach   Water to cover

Chop vegetables fine, or put them through food chopper. Boil them slowly till very soft. For young infants, strain the soup, merely pressing vegetables with back of spoon. For older children press the vegetables through the strainer and use 1 tsp. more of pulp to a small cup of liquid. Water in which rice has been boiled, may be used in place of plain water. For smaller babies, only water in which the vegetables are cooked should be used. Other vegetables may be substituted instead of the ones given. Good ones for children are spinach, chard, lettuce, beets, beet greens, carrots, turnips and celery. These should not be served raw.—Miss Mila Purdy, Oklahoma.

Mexican Chili

2 Tbsp. lard (heaping), allow to melt in sauce pan. When hot add 1 lb. hamburg broken in small pieces; 1 onion chopped. Cover and simmer 20 min. Add: 1 can tomatoes; 1 can red beans or 1 lb. pinto beans soaked over night; salt to taste; 2 tsp. chili powder. Cover and simmer 30 min. longer. Add a little water if tomatoes are thick.—Mrs. Louis Mekota, Iowa.

Clam Chowder

Cut up ⅛ to ¼ lb. salt pork in small pieces and put on in iron skillet to try out. In the meantime have on to cook in a sufficient quantity of water 1 large onion sliced finely and a tomato also sliced. With these cook a level tbsp. rice. When the pork particles are fried crisp mix into the grease 2 tbsp. flour and brown slightly. Then add a little water and 2 or 3 sliced raw potatoes. When potatoes are done, add a small can of minced clams, 1 qt. of milk, and the onion and tomato and rice mixture. Season with pepper and salt as desired and serve with saltines, toast or canapes.—Kathryn G. Woodside, New Mexico.

Potato Soup

2 qt. water   1 qt. chopped potatoes
              2 good sized onions

Cook until done, then add 1 egg into which has been worked 1 small c. flour. Add 1 pt. milk or cream mixed, and salt to taste. Serve very hot with crackers or cubes of toasted bread. —Mrs. J. E. Waggoner, Kansas.

Vegetable Soup

Medium soup bone   1 good sized parsnip
1 good sized carrot   1 small head cabbage
1 small rutabaga   1 medium onion
              4 small potatoes

Put soup bone, not soup meat or rib-boiling, on to cook. Use cold water and bring slowly to boiling point, simmer for 3 hrs. Season with salt and pepper. Prepare vegetables and run thru a food chopper, using coarse knife. When soup bone has been cooking 2 hrs. remove from kettle, pour liquid into another dish, leaving all sediment in kettle. Rinse out and by so doing, you will remove all bones that may have been loosened from the larger bone, as very often happens. Put all back in kettle and add more water, if needed, bring to boil, add vegetables and boil 1 hr. This should make about 3 qts. good rich soup.— Mrs. Warren Kinnear, Wis.

VEGETABLES

Potato Puffs

1 c. mashed potatoes (as for table use)
2 eggs beaten light

1 tsp. salt
1 c. flour
1 rnd. tsp. baking powder

Drop into deep fat and have fat very hot. Cook till quite brown. Drop not more than 1 tbsp. at a time.—Mrs. Arthur Pfolsgrof, Ill.

Mexican Baked Beans

Use red kidney beans. Soak over night. Then drain. Add fresh water and par boil. Cook till tender. To 1 qt. of beans add 2 large tomatoes, 1 onion and 1 green pepper (all chopped) 1 tsp. of salt and 1 of pepper and 2 tbsp. molasses. Cover with water they were boiled in and bake till onions and tomatoes are thoroly done.—Mrs. C. O. Jeffries, Nebr.

Glazed Parsnips

Boil parsnips until almost tender, drain. In a baking dish or pan melt butter or bacon drippings with enough brown sugar to form a syrup. Place parsnips in this, season with salt and pepper and bake slowly until a golden brown. If Parsnips are prepared this way they will rival sweet potatoes.—Mrs. Claude Bishop, Kansas.

Glazed Parsnips

Boil parsnips until almost tender, drain. In a baking dish or pan melt butter or bacon drippings with enough brown sugar to form a syrup. Place parsnips in this, season with salt and pepper and bake slowly until a golden brown. If parsnips are prepared this way they will rival sweet potatoes.—Mrs. Claude Bishop, Kansas.

Greens

If you have a sunny slope on which alfalfa grows real early in spring, gather a mess, prepare just as you would dandelions, or other greens and see what a delicious dish you have; it is excellent, even better than spinach or mustard.—Mrs. Geo. W. Hoyt, Mich.

Vegetables in Casarole

1 c. raw diced potatoes	4 tbsp. chopped onion
1 c. diced celery	¼ c. uncooked rice
1 c. peas	1 c. canned tomatoes
1 c. cooked lima beans	1 tsp. salt

⅛ tsp. pepper

4 bouillion cubes dissolved in 1 c. of boiling water or soup stock. Combine vegetables and season with salt and pepper, place in cassarole and cover with the stock made from bouillion cubes or soup stock. Bake in moderate oven 1 hr.—Mrs. W. F. Zaske, Minn.

Vegetable Pie

1 c. each cooked lima beans, carrots, corn	2 tbsp. minced onion
	2 tbsp. pimento

1 tbsp. butter

Toss lightly together. Put in baking dish, cover with milk, spread mashed potatoes over top and bake to delicate brown in quick oven.—Mrs. P. E. Lewis, Calif.

Baked Tomatoes

Remove thin slices from stem ends of smooth medium sized tomatoes, take out pulp, add bread crumbs or rice, season with salt, pepper and onion juice. Refill the tomatoes with the mixture. Place in buttered pans. Sprinkle with buttered crumbs. Bake 20 min. in hot oven.—Mrs. Arthur Oettinger, Wis.

Escalloped Tomatoes

6 ripe tomatoes	3 c. cracker or dry bread crumbs
1 tbsp. salt	
Dash of pepper	3 tbsp. butter

Little onion if desired

Wash and peel tomatoes. Place a layer of sliced tomatoes in the bottom of the baking dish, sprinkle with cracker crumbs, butter, salt and pepper. Add another layer of tomatoes, cover with crumbs and bits of butter. Bake in moderate oven 20 min. Serve hot.—Frances Adams, Nebr.

Cornish Pasties

Make a short pastry, roll out and line a rather deep pie tin; fill with sliced potatoes and a grating of onion and a layer of meat cut in small pieces. Add pepper and salt and a little water. Cover with pastry and bake in a moderate oven until potatoes are done as can be tested through the slits in upper crust. True cornish pasty has other vegetables in as carrots or turnips. The pasties can be made with fresh meat, or it is a nice way to use a little left over cooked meat; should then have a little drippings of gravy added.—Mrs. Mary Fargher, Mont.

Sweet Potato Puffs

2 c. mashed sweet potatoes, add 2 tbsp. butter, 1 egg beaten light, 1 c. sweet milk. Sift ½ c. flour, 1 tsp. salt and 2 tsp. baking powder. Add to mixture and mix well. Roll ½ c. raisins in flour and add. More flour may be needed to make soft batter. Drop by spoonfuls on greased baking tin and bake until brown.—Mrs. C. S. Carter, Okla.

Baked Squash

1 qt. diced squash	1 tbsp. butter
½ c. cream	¼ c. sugar

Salt and pepper to taste. Bake in rather hot oven for 2 hr.—Mrs. Harry F. Long, Kansas.

Boiled Spinach

Wash spinach, place in kettle. It is not necessary to add any water for cooking, sufficient moisture adheres to the leaves. Cook 12 min. While spinach is cooking slice a medium sized onion in very thin slices. Fry slowly on back of stove in fried meat drippings or butter, until done. Add 1 scant tbsp. flour, brown, then add some milk, let heat, add spinach, a little nutmeg, sprinkle or either red or black pepper and salt to taste. Serve in shallow bowl and top with sliced hard boiled eggs. The onions may be omitted or removed before flour is added.—Mrs. W. C. Hobelman, Okla.

Spanish Rice

Cook in double boiler: 1 c. rice, salt to taste. When tender and dry add: 2 c. tomatoes (strained and cooked). Let simmer ½ hr. together on back of stove, add ¼ lb. grated cheese, 1 tsp. butter, ½ green pepper, 1 tsp. sugar, ¼ tsp. chilipowder (not necessary). Cook all the above together and serve hot. Tomato soup will do in place of the tomatoes.—Mrs. Mildred Cavanaugh, S. Dak.

Stuffed Peppers

To prepare red and green sweep peppers for stuffing, cut off top with knife and remove seeds and veins. The peppers may be filled with a variety of mixtures—chopped cold meats and seasoned bread crumbs and onions, or plain boiled rice. In any and all cases, moisten with melted butter. Stand close together in a dish; pour a little stock or boiling water over them. Bake for 1 hr.—Mrs. Henry Seely, Texas.

Epicure Onions

Boil small onions very tender, salting just before they are done. Drain and place in a shallow pan. Pour over them enough cream sauce to fill chinks well. Grate cheese over, and set in hot oven till golden brown.—Mrs. J. C. Weber, Wis.

Potato Stew

2 qt. diced potatoes placed in kettle with 2 tbsp. grease, 1 c. boiling water, salt to suit taste, add 1 c. diced onions. Cook until tender, and cover with rich milk to depth of 1 in. Add drop dumplings when the moisture is boiling. Make dumplings as follows: 2 c. flour sifted; 4 tsp. baking powder; ½ tsp. salt; 2 tsp. shortening; 1 beaten egg and about ¾ c. milk. Sift dry ingredients. Mix in shortening. Add beaten eggs and milk. Drop in boiling potato mixture. Cover and boil 12 min.—Mrs. Geo. H. Shifflet, Ill.

Stuffed Baked Potatoes

Bake potatoes and cut off tops and remove filling, mix with butter and beaten white of 1 egg, season with salt and pepper and then replace filling in shells, piling it up in a rounded mound. Shake a little paprika on top, set in oven until tops are slightly browned and serve hot garnished with parsley.— Mrs. Fern E. Kelly, Ill.

Novel Baked Potatoes

Peel, boil and mash as many potatoes as needed, add 1 tbsp. butter, salt and pepper, and cream, about 2 or 3 tbsp. cream will be right amount. Place mashed potatoes in buttered baking dish, over potatoes put a large layer of apple sauce, slightly sweetened, and over that criss-cross 6 slices of bacon, when bacon is crisp, (put it in oven to bake) serve in baking dish, at once.—Mrs. J. C. Blake, Ohio.

Creamed Mushrooms

1 lb. mushrooms	2 tbsp. butter
1 large onion	½ tsp. paprika
½ c. cream	½ tsp. salt

Juice of ½ lemon

Select large mushrooms, peel and let stand for ½ hr. in cold water to which you must add the juice of a lemon but not the lemon juice called for in recipe. Drain mushrooms, melt butter in the bottom of a covered dish. Put in a layer of mushrooms covered by a thin layer of sliced onions, and so on until the amounts are used up. Cover closely and let them simmer in a moderate oven until they are cooked soft in their own juices. When soft enough for a fork to pierce easily, add the cream, salt and paprika and let cook for 10 min. longer just before taking to the table add the juice of the ½ lemon. This must be done by carefully sprinkling it over the top. Do not stir after lemon juice is added.—Viola Mahanay, Okla.

Corn and Bacon

Chop 4 slices of bacon in bits and brown slightly and add a No. 2 can of corn, a strip of pimento, if desired, and ¾ tsp. salt, ¼ tsp. pepper and heat thoroly.—Miss Flora Girch, Nebr.

Corn Souffle

1 tbsp. butter	1 can corn
2 tbsp. flour	1 ½ tsp. salt
1 c. milk	⅛ tsp. pepper

2 eggs

Melt butter, mix with flour, and pour milk on gradually. Bring to the boiling point, stirring constantly. Add the corn, seasonings, yolks of eggs well beaten, and the stiffly beaten whites. Turn into buttered dish and bake in a moderate oven, (325°) 30 min. Serve 6.—Mrs. Chas. Oakes, N. Dak.

Hollandaise Celery

1 qt. uncooke dcelery diced, 4 tbsp. butter, 4 egg yolks, ½ tsp. salt, ¼ tsp. pepper, 2 tsp. lemon juice. Cook the celery until tender keeping 2 c. of water in the an. Cream the butter and add salt, pepper and 2 beaten egg yolks, add the other 2 egg yolks beaten and mix well; add to the cooked celery and let stand over hot water on the back of the stove while stirring; add lemon juice. Serve on toast on hot plates.—Addie Folsom, N. H.

Mother's Cauliflower

Place cooked flowerets of cauliflower on serving platter, sprinkle with finely chopped hard boiled egg, minced parsley and buttered bread crumbs, well browned, and salt, pepper and bits of butter. Serve hot.—Mrs. J. C. Weber, Wis.

Glazed Carrots

12 med. sized carrots, par-boiled until tender	¼ c. water
	4 tbsp. lard
½ c. granulated sugar	2 tbsp. chopped parsley

Dissolve sugar in water and add to lard, in cold frying pan. Heat until lard is melted. Add carrots and parsley and cook until carrots are glazed but not browned. Serve on platter, garnish with a few fresh parsley leaves. Serve 6 persons. Parsnips may be prepared in the same way.—Mrs. Chas. Sewing, Ia.

Carrot Newburg

1 pt. cream sauce	1 tbsp. minced onion
(See page)	1 tsp. chopped parsley
2 tbsp. minced green sweet	2 c. diced cooked carrots
peppers	

Add peppers, onion and parsley to cream sauce. Pour over diced carrots and sprinkle with parsley and serve.—Mrs. Willie Inderlied, Nebr.

Scalloped Cabbage

2 c. cooked cabbage	¼ lb. cheese
1 c. white sauce	Dash of pepper
(See page)	

Shred cabbage, place in kettle and boil for 20 min in salt water. Mix ¾ of the cheese and white sauce, arrange alternately layers of cabbage and sauce in buttered baking dish. Cover with butter, bread crumbs and sprinkle with the remainder of the cheese, which has been grated. Bake in hot oven till brown.—Mrs. Flora Helbert, Ind.

Green Style Cabbage

Cut a small cabbage into 1 inch slices, crosswise. Soak in salted water ½ hr. Cook till tender in 2 c. water, ½ c. olive oil, ⅓ c. lemon juice, 6 peppercorns, 2 bay leaves, ¼ tsp. thyme, 1 tsp. salt, 4 tsp. sugar, and 1 c. diced celery. Serve hot.—Mrs. J. C. Weber, Wis.

Sauer Kraut and Dumplings

Boil sauer kraut and lean pork until pork is tender, 15 min. before serving, add the dumplings made as follows:

2 c. flour	1 tsp. salt
2 tsp. baking powder	1 egg
⅔ c. milk	

Sift dry ingredients, add egg and milk. Drop by spoonfuls into the kettle. Keep tightly covered 12 min.—Mrs. W. A. Parsons, Kansas.

Buttered Beets

Mix 4 tbsp brown sugar	4 tbsp. vinegar
with	1 tsp. salt
¼ tsp. pepper	

Boil till thick then add 2 tbsp. butter. Mix this thoroly and pour over 3 c. young beets which have been cut in small pieces after cooking. Set in oven 10 min. before serving.—Norma Walter, Minn.

String Beans

Method No. 1: Boil till done in salt water. Do not drain the beans after cooking them. Make a good salad dressing using mustard. Add one medium sized onion, cut fine and the hot dressing using a little more flour to make the consistency of gravy.

Method No. 2: Boil in water and drain. Cut bacon in cubes and fry till crisp and add a small amount of onion, put in beans and smother till beans are browned.—Mrs. John L. Boettcher, Minn.

Baked Beans (Picnic)

1 qt. navy beans
½ lb. sliced bacon
1 tsp. mustard

1 tbsp. brown sugar
1 tsp. ginger
2 tbsp. molasses

1 tbsp. salt

Soak beans over night. In morning add 1 tsp. soda and boil till soft. Drain. Add fresh water, mustard, sugar, molasses, ginger, salt and bacon. Bake slowly till done. Requires about 3 hr.—Mrs. Holger Johnson, Minn.

Creamed Asparagus on Toast

1 small can asparagus
2 c. white sauce

6 pieces crisp toast
¼ c. grated cheese

Heat the asparagus in the liquid in which it was canned by placing over slow fire. Place the hot asparagus on the crisp toast and pour over it the hot white sauce. Sprinkle with grated cheese, set in an oven until cheese melts. Garnish with paprika and parsley. Serve hot.—Mrs. Chas. Oakes, N. Dak.

Baked Egg Plant

1 egg plant
1 small onion
1 small pepper

1 egg
1 c. bread crumbs
1 tsp. salt

Dice and boil egg plant, pepper and onions in salt water until tender. Drain and mash. Beat in egg while hot. Thicken with part of bread crumbs. Pour in baking dish. Sprinkle with bread crumbs, and dot with butter. Bake in moderate oven about ½ hr.—Mrs. W. A. Moore Mississippi.

Sweet Potatoes With Pineapple

4 large sweet potatoes
4 slices pineapple

½ c. brown sugar
½ c. pineapple juice

2 tbsp. butter

Slice the sweet potatoes (boiled) in a shallow baking dish after rubbing in a little salt. Over them spread the diced pineapple. Boil the sugar, pineapple juice and butter 3 min. and pour over the potato and pineapple and bake 20 min. in a hot oven, basting three times with the juice in the an.—Addie Folsom, N. H.

Potato Timballs

2 c. mashed potato	2 tbsp. butter
½ c. milk	2 eggs

Salt, pepper, chopped parsley

Mash potatoes, add milk, butter and eggs slightly beaten. Season with salt, pepper and a little chopped parsley. Put into buttered dish and bake until firm in a moderate oven (350°) for 30 min. Serve 6.—Mrs. Chas Oakes, N. Dak.

Hot Slaw

1 head cabbage	Salt and pepper
2 tbsp. butter	⅓ c. vinegar
2 tbsp, chopped onion	1 c. cream
Water	1 egg

Melt butter, add chopped onion; cook for 3 min. then add sliced cabbage. Cook slowly 5 min. Add about 1 inch of water in stewing kettle, let simmer until tender. Sprinkle salt and pepper. Add the cream to which has been added the well beaten egg and vinegar. Bring to boiling point. Serve.— Florence McGlashan, N. Y.

DESSERTS, HOT AND COLD

Jerusalem Pudding

Soak ½ package gelatine in ¼ c. cold water. When dissolved pour over this ½ c. boiling water, cool. Add this to 1 pt. whipped cream. To this add:

½ c. sugar	½ c. figs and dates
⅔ c. cooked rice	½ c. nut meats

1 tsp. vanilla

Mix well, set in cold place until chilled. Add any kind of fruit wished.—Mrs. Ray M. Johnson, Nebraska.

Stuffed Angel Food Cake

Bake an angel food using recipe on page ( ). Cut inside of cake, leaving a 2 inch rim. Also leave an inch thickness at bottom of cake. Fill with following stuffing.

1 c. nuts	½ lb. marshmallows
1 c. diced pineapple	(diced)
1 c. cocoanut	12 marachino cherries
	(small bottle

One-half the cherries may be used on top the cake. Mix this with the inside if the cake which has been torn in small pieces. Fill the cake shell. Let stand in ice box at least 12 hrs. Cover with whipped cream and the cherries and slice and serve.—Mrs. C. D. McLain, Missouri.

Danish Dessert

Use rye or graham bread. 1 qt. bread crumbs; 1½ tbsp. butter, put in spider and fry lightly; crumbs should be light, not greasy. 1 qt. good apple sauce, not too much juice, but enough to soak crumbs. Just sweeten a little and put in layers on plate. Two layers of each alternaely, sauce and crumbs. When ready to serve put whipped cream on top and garnish with some kind of clear jelly. It looks rich and will taste just as good.—Mrs. Wm. Maier, North Dakota.

Graham Cracker Tarts

1 c. butter	1½ c. milk
2 c. sugar	40 graham crackers
6 eggs (whites and yolks	4 tsp. baking powder
beaten separate)	2 c. chopped nuts

1 tsp. vanilla

Cream butter and sugar. Add yolks and milk. Mix baking powder crackers, and nuts. Add to first mixture, then add vanilla. Fold in whites beaten stiff. Bake in quick oven (400 degrees).—Mrs. Arthur Oettinger, Wisconsin.

Delicious Angel Food, Ala American

Beat the whites of 6 eggs, till frothy, add 1 tsp. cream tartar. Beat until smooth as velvet, sift in gradually 1 c. sugar, sift ¾ c. cake flour 6 times, and fold in lightly, bake in 2 pans. Then take 1 envelope gelatine, color it real red with fruit color or cherry juice and add juice from 1 lemon, 1 c. sugar, 1 pt. water, heat all together when cool, before it sets fill with pineapple, cherry preserves, any other fruit you like. When it is set and real solid turn it between the angel food it should be as thick as each layer of cake. Slice when ready to serve and pile a large amount of whipped cream on each slice. This is delicious as well as a beautiful dessert. I use the same pan I baked the cake in to mould the gelatine as it must be the same size as cake.—Mrs. T. P. Lyman, Missouri.

Crow's Nest Dessert

Melt butter size of an egg in a pudding dish. Peel and slice 6 large apples and cover with 1 c. sugar. Make a batter of the following: 1 c. sour cream; add a pinch of soda and a pinch of salt to the cream. Add flour enough to make a thin batter and pour over apples and bake 1 hr. Serve with cream and sugar.—Mrs. I. Gorden, North Dakota.

Cherry Pudding

First part:

1 c. flour	1 tsp salt
¾ c. sugar	2 tsp. butter
1 tsp. baking powder	½ c. cold water

Second part:

1 c. cherries	½ c. sugar, or more if
1½ c. boiling water	cherries are very sour
½ c. sugar, or	

Pour first part in baking pan and spread in cherries. Sprinkle the sugar on and pour on the boiling water and bake. Serve with cream and sugar.—Mrs. A. J. Hubbait, Illinois.

Cranberry Roly Poly

2 c. flour	¾ c. milk
4 tsp. baking powder	4 c. cranberries
½ tsp. salt	2½ c. sugar
2 tbsp. shortening	1 c. water

Cook cranberries, water and sugar together. Make a biscuit dough of the flour, making powder, salt, shortening and milk. Roll out dough to ¼ inch thickness. Spread ¾ of cooked cranberries on this, using as little juice as possible. Roll up into a roll. Place on a pan and steam ½ hr. When done slice and serve with sauce made of the cranberries left over, putting together the juice and cranberries and 1 tbsp. flour then cooked until thick.—Bertha A. DeMotte, Indiana.

Fig Pudding

1 c. chopped figs   ¾ c. sugar
1 c. grated suet   ½ tsp. salt
1½ c. flour   1 c. milk

Grate suet, and mix well with salt, flour, sugar and milk, add the chopped figs, put into cloth, tie tight, leaving some room to swell, and boil 3 hrs. Serve with hot sauce as follows: 1 tbsp. flour; 1 tbsp. cornstarch; 1 level tsp. butter; salt and sugar to suit taste. Mix with little milk till smooth, then add ½ c. boiling water, then add 1 c. milk and boil 10 min. Put sugar and salt and butter in a bowl and pour over the hot sauce.—Mrs. W. C. Greenfield, Pennsylvania.

Vanilla Wafer Dessert

Beat well together the following:
4 egg yolks   ½ c. orange juice
1 tbsp. lemon juice   ⅔ c. sugar
Grated rind of 1 lemon   Pinch salt

Cook in double boiler until thick and add 4 egg whites beaten still. When cool, fold in ½ c. whipped cream. Pour into pan to set. Cover with vanilla wafer crumbs.—Mrs. H. E. Tweedy, Nebraska.

Sailors Duff

2 tbsp. butter   ½ c. molasses
2 tbsp. sugar   ½ c. boiling water
1 egg   1½ c. flour.
¼ tsp. salt

1 tsp. soda sifted in flour. Mix as for cake, beat thoroughly. Steam 1 hr. Serve with following sauce: 3 tbsp. sugar (rounded) 1 tbsp. flour(heaping). Mix well and add butter the size of walnut. Then add 1½ c. boiling water. Let boil and add lemon extract.—Mrs. C. E. Hammer, Illinois.

Raspberry Meringue

Whites of 3 eggs, ¼ tsp. vanilla, 3 tsp. baking powder, 1¼ c. sugar. Beat egg whites until stiff and dry. Add gradually ⅔ of sugar and beat until mixture holds shape. Fold in remaining sugar sifted with baking powder. Add vanilla. Drop by spoonfuls on unglazed paper. Bake in moderate oven for 25-30 min. Remove any soft places from meringues and return to oven to dry out after heat is turned off. Use 2 meringues for each serving and put together with sweetened whipped cream and crushed raspberries.—Ruth I. Jones, South Dak.

Prune Whip

8 large prunes soaked in   Boil until tender
     water, or ⅓ lb.   1 c. sugar
7 egg whites

Drain prunes, chop fine. Beat whites stiff, add sugar, pinch of cream tartar. Add prunes, put into buttered dish set in pan of hot water. Bake 30 min. Serve with cream.—Mrs. Oliver Smock, Wisconsin.

English Plum Pudding

1 c. suet	1 c. raisins, (floured)
1 tsp. cinnamon	1 c. bread crumbs
1 tsp. nutmeg	1 c. sugar
1 c. molasses	1 c. sweet milk

1 tbsp. soda

Chop suet fine, to this add bread crumbs, spices, sugar, molasses, raisins, dissolve soda in milk. Beat all together. Add enough flour to make stiff batter. Pour into cloth that has been wet and sprinkled with flour. Boil 2½ hrs. in kettle of boiling water. Serve with hard sauce.—Mrs. W. J. Rathke, Minnesota.

Date Nut Pudding

1 lb. dates	1½ c. bread crumbs
1½ c. shortening	1½ c. flour
1½ c. nuts	½ c. milk
¾ c. sugar	1 egg

2 tsp. baking powder

Cut dates in small pieces. Grind nuts. Mix in other ingredients and bake in moderate oven. Serve with whipped cream.—Mrs. R. E. Batman, Kansas.

French Caramel Custard

First prepare the sauce. Select two pans, one smaller than the other, as for boil custard. To ½ c. sugar add 2 tbsp. water, place over fire and boil until it becomes a golden brown. Do not burn. Remove from fire and turn the pan so as to coat the sides as well as the bottom with the sauce. When cold it is ready to add the custard. To prepare the custard: 4 eggs well beaten, 8 tbsp. sugar and 4 c. sweet milk. Mix well and pour into prepared pan. Place in pan of hot water, put in oven and cook until set. If individual custard cups are desired prepare the sauce as stated above and pour into the cups before putting in the custard.—Miss Iva Swofford, Arizona.

Caramel Dumplings

For syrup:	
Burn 1 c. sugar to a light brown, add:	Pinch salt
	1 tsp. vanilla
2½ c. boiling water	1 tbsp. butter
For batter:	
½ c. sugar	1 tsp. baking powder
1 tbsp. butter	1 tsp. vanilla
Mix to cream and add:	½ c. sweet milk
Pinch salt	Flour to make real stiff

Drop batter in syrup, brown in oven and serve with cream. —Mrs. Henry Loyd, Missouri.

Carrot Pudding

½ c. butter	1 c. sugar
1 c. grated carrots	2 c. flour
1 c. grated potatoes	1 tsp. soda
1 c. raisins	1 tsp. cloves
1 c. currants	1 tsp. cinnamon

Cream butter and sugar. Sift dry ingredients. Combine with grated carrots and potatoes, raisins and currants. Add to the butter mixture. Place in buttered cans and steam 2 hrs.— Mrs. Ray Kopischke, North Dakota.

Snow Pudding

4 c. milk	4 tbsp. cornstarch
1 c. sugar	¼ tsp. salt

Boil thick in double boiler and let cool and stir in 4 well beaten egg whites, 1 tsp. vanilla. Sauce of pudding: ⅔ c. sweet cream; 1 c. milk, let come to boiling point in double boiler, stir in 4 well beaten egg yolks with ½ c. sugar and ½ tsp. lemon extract. Pinch of salt. Serve cold.—Mrs. H. A. Ayer, Kansas.

Baked Apple Rolls

2 c. flour	1 tsp. salt
2 tsp. baking powder	2 tbsp. lard
¾ c. sweet milk	

Sift dry ingredients and mix liquids and then combine the two. Roll ¼ in. thick and spread with sliced apples; sprinkle with sugar and cinnamon, roll like jelly roll, slice 1 in. thick, set in greased pan. Mix the following:

½ c. corn syrup	2 c. cold water
¾ c. sugar	2 tbsp. butter
1½ tbsp. cornstarch	little nutmeg

Pour over apple rolls and bake till light brown. Serve hot or cold.—Mrs. E. Howe, Canada.

Apricot Jello

Cook ¼ lb. apricots until soft, rub thru a colander and sweeten to taste. Dissolve 1 package of orange jello in 1 pt. of hot water and when nearly cold, stir the apricots into the jello. Set away until cold and firm.—Thelma Zerfas, Kansas.

Baked Bananas

4 bananas	Juice of 1 lemon
½ c. sugar	2 tbsp. butter
¼ c. water	

Peal and scrape the bananas, then cut into halves lengthth-wise. Place in a shallow baking pan and pour over them ½ the sauce—made by cooking the remaining ingredients. Bake in a moderate oven for about 20 min. When half thru baking process add the remaining sauce. Serve with whipped cream.—Mrs. Chas. Oakes, North Dakota.

Cocoanut Bread Pudding

6 slices bread	1 pt. milk
2 eggs	4 tbsp. sugar
½ tsp. salt	1 c. cocoanut

Soak bread in water until soft. Drain off water, add milk, eggs, sugar and salt. Beat well, add cocoanut. Put in a buttered baking dish and grate or sprinkle a little nutmeg over the top. Dot with butter. Bake until firm in moderate oven. Serve with hard sauce. A cup of raisins may be added.—Mrs. Bernard G. Hessel, Minnesota.

Angel Food Pudding

2 eggs	1 tsp. baking powder
1 c. powdered sugar	1 c. broken nut meats
1 tsp. flour	1 c. dates

Beat the egg yolks until creamy, add powdered sugar, flour and baking powder sifted together. Fold in egg whites beaten stiff, add nuts and dates. Set in a pan of boiling water and bake about 45 min. in a medium oven. Let cool, serve with whipped cream.—Clara Morris, Iowa.

Pineapple Tapioca Whip

1 c. min. tapioca	1 small can crushed pine-
2 qt. boiling water	apple
Pinch salt	1 tsp. extract
1 c. sugar	1 c. whipped cream

Place tapioca, water and salt in double boiler, cook till thickens. Take out and cool. Add 1 c. sugar, pineapple and flavoring. Mix whipped cream just before serving.—Mrs. Jack Rosenheimer, Indiana.

Baked Custard

4 eggs	4 tbsp. sugar
3 c. milk	⅛ tsp. salt
	1 tsp. vanilla

Scald milk, heat eggs well, add sugar, salt and scalded milk. Strain into custard cups or deep dish. Grate a little nutmeg over the top. Set in a pan of hot water and bake very slowly in a moderate oven until firm. Test by running a knife thru custard. If it comes out clean the custard is done. Do not let the water, surrounding the mold boil or custard will turn to whey.—Etta Kirkland. North Carolina.

Swimming Swans

Place 4 c. milk in double boiler, let boil and add ¾ c. sugar, 4 tbsp. cornstarch, which have been mixed together. When cooked pour over the whites of 3 eggs which have been beaten very stiff.—Mrs. Ed McIntyre, Illinois.

Caramel Apple Tapioca

½ c. min. tapioca	3 apples (sliced)
¼ tsp. salt	½ c. raisins
½ c. brown sugar	¼ c. sugar
2 c. hot water	¼ tsp. cinnamon

2 tbsp. butter

Cook the tapioca, salt, sugar and water in a double boiler; put the apples and the raisins in a greased baking dish, sprinkle over with the second amount of sugar, nutmeg and butter, pour tapioca mixture over all and bake in a moderate oven (375 degrees) until the apples are soft (about 25 min.) Serve hot or cold with whipped or plain cream or you may have a meringue browned on top of this pudding.—Alma C. Hollman, Missouri.

Chocolate Pudding

1 qt. milk	2 eggs
1½ c. sugar	6 tbsp. flour

3 tbsp. chocolate or cocoa

Heat milk, and beaten eggs, mix sugar, flour and cocoa dry, add to hot milk, beat till all the lumps are smooth, cook till thick, put in dish cut marshmellows on top.—Mrs. J. C. Johnson, Iowa.

Caramel Pudding

Use 1 can sweetened condensed milk and boil 2 hrs. Remove from can and add ½ c. nuts and serve in sherbet glasses with whipped cream.—Mrs. Fred H. Shrader, Wisconsin.

Strawberry Surprise

2½ c. preserved straw- berries	3 c. boiled rice Italian Cream

Add 1 c. berries to boiled rice and beat in double boiler until rice has absorbed juice of berries. Put rice into greased molds or deep round cake pan. Set in ice-box to chill for 3 hrs. When ready to serve, unmold, or serving plate, and cover with Italian cream. Garnish with the larger berries. To serve, cut in slices like cake and over each slice pour some of the remaining fruit.

Italian Cream:

1½ c. sugar	2 egg whites
½ c. water	1 c. whipping cream

Cook sugar and water together in sauce pan. Stir until sugar is dissolved. Continue cooking until syrup spins a thread. Pour slowly over the well-beaten egg whites, beating constantly, while adding. Continue beating until cool. Fold in stiffly beaten cream. Spread thickly over rice mold. This Italian cream is less sweet than frosting and more flavorsome than whipped cream.—Mrs. W. L. West, Colorado.

Strawberry Shortcake

2 c. flour	½ tsp. salt
2 tbsp. sugar	3 tbsp. shortening
4 tsp. baking powder	1 egg

½ c. milk

Sift flour, sugar, baking powder, and salt. Cut in shortening. Add beaten egg to milk and stir into dry ingredients, to make soft dough. Divide and smooth out lightly. Bake in deep greased layer tins in hot oven until light brown. Split and spread between layers crushed sweetened fresh or canned strawberries. Cover top with whipped cream and more berries. About ½ pt. whipping cream will make enough.—Mrs. W. A. Puterbaugh, Indiana.

ICE CREAM

Fresh Peach Ice Cream

Make a boiled custard of 2 c. milk and
⅔ c. sugar and 1 tsp. cornstarch and 2
eggs, well beaten, ¼ tsp. salt. Mix sugar
and salt and cornstarch and add well
beaten eggs. Scald milk in double boiler
and pour over mixture. Return to double
boiler and stir constantly until mixture
is thick enough to coat a spoon. Cool,
flavor with 2 tsp. vanilla extract. Add 2
c. fresh peaches, which have been peeled
and crushed and sweetened with 1 c.
powdered sugar. Add 1 tsp. lemon juice.
Just before freezing stir in 1 c. cream.
—Mrs. Bayard Johnson, Nebraska.

Orange Ice Cream

8 oranges (grate some of the rind)
2 lemons, juice through strainer
5 c. sugar
1 qt. cream
3 qt. milk
Freeze
    —Mrs. Harry Bohl, Colorado.

Walnut Brittle Ice Cream

2 c. granulated sugar
2 c. broken English
   walnuts
2 doz. dry macaroons
1 qt. milk

1 c. light brown sugar
2 eggs
1 c. heavy cream
Few grains salt

Melt sugar in iron or heavy aluminum spider, stirring constantly over a low fire. When sugar is a thin syrup add nuts.
Turn onto a well buttered platter or sheet and spread thin.
When cool and hard put through food chopper. Crumble
macaroons and toast in a hot oven for 5 min. Combine and
thoroughly mix the chopped brittle and macaroons. Scalt milk
in top of double boiler. Beat eggs slightly with brown sugar
and slowly add hot milk, stirring constantly. Return to double
boiler and cook over hot water until custard coats a metal
spoon. Let cool and add cream whipped until firm. Turn into
freezer and freeze with or without stirring. When half frozen
add about ¾ of the nut and macaroon mixture, saving the
rest to sprinkle over the cream when serving. Finish freezing
and pack in a mold to ripen for 1 hr. or longer.—Mrs. B. M.
Elmore, Vermont.

Peppermint Ice Cream

1 ¼ lb. red and white stick candy, peppermint
1 qt. new milk   1 ½ c. thick cream

Soak the stick candy in the new milk overnight. Then in morning add the thick cream. Stir well and freeze for 5 hrs.— Mary M. Auselin, Missouri.

Cranberry Ice

1 qt. cranberries   1 lb. sugar
1 pt. water   Juice of 2 lemons

Cook cranberries with water until tender, strain, then add sugar and cook until dissolved, cool, add lemon juice and freeze. Use 3 parts of ice to 1 part of salt for freezing.— Rush E. Hanna, Kansas.

Apricot Sherbet

Boil 3 c. sugar and 1 qt. water for 5 min. Cool and add 1 can of apricots that have been put through the colander, and the juice of 2 lemons. When partly frozen, add 1 pt. thick cream. Finish freezing as other creams. This quantity makes 1 gallon.—Mrs. Harley Montgomery, Mo.

Plum Juice Ice

1 qt. plum juice   1 c. cold water
2 c. sugar   ½ c. cream

Mix juice, water and sugar, stirring constantly while cream is added slowly. Freeze at once. This makes a delightfully refreshing purplish-pink ice.—Mrs. Samie Lee Cox, Kentucky.

Delight Caramel Ice Cream

1 qt. cream   1 egg
2 c. milk   1 tbsp. flour
1 ⅓ c. sugar   ⅛ tbsp. salt
2 tbsp. vanilla

Mix flour, sugar and salt, add egg slightly beaten and add milk gradually. Cook over hot water 20 min. Stir constantly at first. ½ sugar is used in custard, remaining ½ carmelized and added slowly to hot custard. Strain and freeze. This recipe may also be used for a plain custard ice cream, without carmelizing sugar. 1 qt. strawberries may be substituted in place of carmelized sugar.—Gertie L. Ritterman, North Dakota.

Ice Cream

4 eggs   1 qt. milk
2 c. sugar   1 qt. thin cream
1 tbsp. vanilla

Mix eggs and sugar, then add cream, milk and vanilla, then beat with egg beater till sugar is all dissolved. Makes just the right amount for a 3 qt. freezer.—Mrs. Oscar Burnell, Iowa.

Ice Cream

1 qt. fresh whole milk,   1 c. cream
    lukewarm   1⅓ c. sugar

Put in freezer, dissolve 1 junket tablet in 1 tbsp. cold water. Stir this into freezer and mix all well. Let stand till jellied. Then add 1 tbsp. vanilla and freeze. Serve with butterscotch sauce. Butter Scotch Sauce: 1 c. cream, 1 c. sugar, 1 c. syrup (colored). Let boil up well, then add 1 tbsp. butter and ½ tsp. vanilla, serve on ice cream.—Mrs. F. L. Hendrixson, Kansas.

Cocoa Syrup

For Ice Cream, Puddings, etc.
1 c. cocoa   2 c. boiling water
2 c. sugar   Dash of salt
        2 tsp. vanilla

Mix cocoa, sugar and salt. Add boiling water and stir well. Boil 25 min. Remove from fire and add vanilla. Cool and place in sterilized jars; seal and keep in refrigerator until ready for use.—Emma Blecha, Missouri.

SALADS AND SALAD DRESSINGS

Salads to be good must be cold. Unless directions for salad state differently, do not combine them until just before ready to serve. Drain the juice from all fruits and vegetables before combining them into salads. Use a wire sieve for draining. Left over vegetables, fruits, meats, may be combined into salads which are delicious and healthful.

Thousand Island Dressing

1 c. stiff mayonnaise
⅔ c. chilli sauce
¼ c. cucumber pkls., sweet
1 hard boiled egg
Grated onion to taste
2 green peppers (chopped)
1 tbsp. parsley (chopped)
¼ c. nuts (chopped)

Season with salt, sugar and paprika ⅓ c. whipped cream may be added if desired.—Mrs. H. A. Fearey, Utah.

Vegetable Salad (Serves 12)

1 small head cabbage, fluted or shredded coarse
1 bunch celery hearts, diced
1 large cucumber fluted med. thick
12 small even sized tomatoes
1 large green sweet pepper
12 small slices, Bermuda onion
12 large crisp leaves lettuce
12 sprigs curly parsley
12 thin slices stuffed olives
12 small radishes   Dash paprika
Serve with Russian or plain dressing

Marinate cabbage and celery with heavy dressing. Arrange lettuce on salad plates, make nest of cabbage and celery and place tomato in center. Cut ¼ or ⅛ nearly through to form flower. Drop bits of dressing and place sliced olives over parsley in center of flower. Arrange 1 slice of onion and cucumber, 1 radish with green tip on plate to suit fancy. Sprinkle with finely shredded or diced green and red peppers over all and dash paprika over all. All ingredients should be chilled. This may be served on large chop plates, which makes attractive decorations for covered dish luncheons.—Beulah Hauser, Iowa.

Fruit Twenty-Four Hour Salad

1 can pineapple
1 pt. cream, whipped
½ lb. marshmallows
¼ lb. nuts
1 can white cherries, seeded

Put the following dressing in the whipped cream:

4 egg yolks
2 lemons (juice of)
1 tsp. sugar
Pinch of salt

Little mustard

Cook in double boiler. After the dressing has been added to the cream, add the fruit and let stand over night.—Mrs. C. E. Hammer, Illinois.

Russian Salad

Cover a box of gelatine with half a pint of cold water and let soak ½ hr. Add 1 pt. boiling water, the juice of 2 lemons, 1 tsp. salt and a dash of red pepper. Let cool, but not congeal. Dip a mold in cold water, put on the bottom a layer of cooked peas, then a layer of diced cooked potatoes, then 2 hard cooked eggs, sliced, then a layer cold meat, ground or sliced, or a layer of nuts. Sprinkle with salt and pepper. Cover with another layer of peas, and finish with a layer of sardines. Pour over all the cooled gelatine and set aside to harden. Serve in slices with mayonnaise dressing or with whipped cream into which a little grated horseradish has been mixed.—Mrs. Lelia Munsell, Kansas.

Cranberry Salad

2 c. cranberries
2 c. sugar
1 c. chopped uncooked apples
1 c. chopped nuts
½ c. chopped celery
3 tbsp. orange juice

Cook cranberries until done, remove from fire and cool; run through colander. Now add equal parts of sugar and pulp; return to fire and jell. Then mix with rest of ingredients. Mayonnaise dressing can be used on this and omit the orange juice. I do not care for the dressing with cranberries. This is an excellent salad served with chicken. Especially pressed chicken sandwiches.—Miss Pauline Frazier, Missouri.

Kidney Bean Salad

1 can or equal amount of red kidney beans
4 sweet pickles, cut fine
½ c. celery cut fine
4 hard boiled eggs
2 small onions cut fine
Boiled salad dressing
Mix well together

—Mrs. Ben L. Vondra, Colorado.

Macaroni Salad

Boil ½ lb. macaroni in salt water till tender. When cold add, chopped::

1 small onion
2 stalks celery
½ small sweet pepper

1 carrot
½ cucumber
4 hard boiled eggs

Add salt and pepper and favorite mayonnaise. Serve on lettuce.—Mrs. Esther Miller, Ohio.

Chicken Salad

3 c. cold chicken, diced
1½ c. celery, cut fine
¼ c. chopped green peppers or pimentos

2 hard boiled eggs
1½ c. mayonnaise
1 head lettuce shredded

Mix chicken, celery and pepper and chill. Before serving mix with dressing and arrange on lettuce. Garnish with white and yolks of eggs to look like daisies.—Mrs. Arthur Jones, Missouri.

Delicious Chicken Salad With Jello

Stew a nice fat chicken until tender. When cool, pick meat off the bones and separate meat from skin, cut the meat in small pieces. 1 pt. chicken broth; 3 tbsp. vinegar or lemon juice, dissolve in 1 package of lemon jello. When jello is cool and partly congealed add the following:

1 c. chicken meat
1 c. celery diced or
  shredded cabbage
1 pimento

1 c. chopped nut meats
1 green pepper or crisp
  pickle

Place in individual moulds or in one mould, which ever you prefer, and place in a cool place until ready to serve. When you will turn salad on individual salad plates or salad dish as you wish to serve it and garnish with lettuce leaves and halves of nuts.—Mrs. O. L. Shults, Kansas.

Veal Salad

2 c. cold diced veal
1 c. diced celery
½ c. canned peas
3 hard boiled eggs

3 tbsp. olive oil
2 tbsp. vinegar
½ tsp. salt
⅛ tsp. pepper

Combine, veal, celery, peas, anl eggs chopped fine. Mix the olive oil, vinegar, salt and pepper to make a dressing marinate the ingredients with the dressing. Serve on lettuce leaves with any salad dressing desired.—Mrs. Pearl E. Pearson, Arizona.

Cabbage Salad

1 pt. shredded cabbage
1 onion
2 apples

1 tsp. celery seed
1 c. raisins
Mix with dressing
—Mrs. E. O. Stockton. Ark.

Salmon Salad

1 can salmon	6 hard boiled eggs
4 boiled potatoes	Small quantity celery
2 dill pickles (chopped	Onion if desired
fine)	Season to taste

Combine with any good cooked salad dressing. Adding eggs last. Let stand a few hours before serving.—Mrs. Mildred Cavanaugh, South Dakota.

Mystery Salad

1 c. shrimps	½ c. French dressing
¼ c. diced pineapple	¼ tsp. curry powder
¼ c. chopped green pepper	2 hard boiled egg yolks

Marinate shrimps in French dressing seasoned with curry powder. Add pineapple, pepper and riced egg yolks. Serve in a hallowed out apple or on a cabbage leaf, garnish with mayonnaise and sprinkle with capers.—Juanita Beauton, Texas.

Tomato and Fish Salad

Peel medium sized tomatoes, remove a thin slice from the tops and take out seeds and pulp. Mix cold boiled fish (or a good quality red salmon) with half the amount of cold boiled potatoes chopped fine, season with salt, pepper and chopped celery and onion if preferred, green sweet peppers may also be added. Moisten with a mayonnaise dressing, fill the tomatoes with the mixture, put 1 tsp. of mayonnaise dressing on top and serve on lettuce leaves.—Mrs. W. K. Evans, Kansas.

Vegetable Salad

2 c. chopped celery	1 c. ground or grated car-
2 c. chopped cabbage	rots
3 sweet pickles	1 pkg. lemon jello

Season the cabbage, celery and carrots with salt and also sprinkle a little sugar over the cabbage. When the jello is cool, add the vegetables. Put in molds and let set. Serve on lettuce with mayonnaise dressing.—Mrs. Geo. E. Rossman, Illinois.

Potato Salad

1 qt. boiled, cubed potatoes
4 hard boiled eggs, coarsely chopped
2 onions, chopped or ground fine
1 tbsp. melted butter
Celery, cut into small pieces
1 medium sized cucumber, seeded and cubed
1 or 2 tbsp. mayonnaise or thousand island dressing, boiled
dressing, pepper, salt, vinegar and cream to taste.

Combine as follows: A layer each of potatoes, celery and eggs, seasoning each layer with onion, salt and pepper. Mix in butter and a little cream and vinegar. Add boiled salad dressing to taste and let-stand for at least an hour. Just before serving add cucumber and mayonnaise or thousand island dressing. If necessary thin with cream, and if not sufficient acid add vinegar.—Mrs. J. Loesges, Illinois.

Peanut Brittle Salad

1 pt. whipping cream	1 box marshmallows
½ lb. peanut brittle	

Grind peanut brittle on food chopper. Mix and let stand a while. This is a delicious salad quick and easy to make.—Mrs. Clyde E. Miller, Missouri.

Pineapple and Cheese Salad

1 pkg. lemon jello	1 c. whipped cream
1 c. shredded, drained pineapple	1 c. boiling water
	½ c. grated cheese

Put contents of jello in a bowl, pour on boiling water. Stir well. Set in a cool place. When the jello starts to congeal, whip with dover egg beater until it gets like whipped egg whites. Add the whipped cream, pineapple and cheese. Mix and pour in a mold to harden. Serve on lettuce with mayonnaise dressing. (A tbsp. each of chopped celery and green pepper added to the mayonnaise improves it).—Mrs. Ernest A. Swanson, Nebraska.

Cottage Cheese Salad

For the foundation use:	A little minced onion and celery
1 qt. cottage cheese	
2 hard boiled eggs	Vegetables may be used
Salt and pepper to taste	Nuts if desired

Mix the whole of ingredients and make a smooth mixture by addition of rich cream. Garnish with lettuce, if liked sweet use sugar to suit taste. This is good sandwich spread also.— Mrs. Herman Ellis, Illinois.

Health Salad

½ c. each celery, apple, nuts, carrots, raisins, cut fine. Serve on crisp lettuce with orange or lemon juice; mayonnaise or French dressing.—Mrs. P. E. Lewis, California.

Quick Salad Dressing

2 egg yolks or 1 whole egg	1 tsp. sugar
2 tbsp. vinegar	½ tsp. mustard
2 tbsp. lemon juice	1 c. vegetable oil
1 ¼ tsp. salt	Few grains of cayenne

Put all together in a mixing bowl and beat together. Prepare a paste of ⅓ c. flour, 1 c. water and 1 tbsp. butter, and mix the three thoroughly and cook until it is a thick paste. At once, add it to the eggs and oil mixture. Beat all together with Dover egg beater until a uniform dressing results.—Mrs. H. A. Fearey, Utah.

MARMALADES, JAMS AND JELLIES

Orange Marmalade

1 doz. oranges
¼ doz. lemons

3 qt. water
8 lb. sugar

Slice the fruit very thin, cutting each slice int three or four pieces. Remove all the seeds. Turn the water over it and let it stand for 24 hrs. Then boil 2 or 3 hrs., or until tender. Add the sugar and boil ½ hr. longer. Turn into tumblers and when cold, cover as you do jelly or jam. Keep in a cool place.—Miss Ragnhild Fredrickson, Wisconsin.

Italian Prune Conserve

3 lb. prunes, pitted but do not peel, run thru a coarse food chopper; 3 lb. sugar. Cook slowly till fruit is preserved and add 1 lb. raisins and 2 c. chopped English walnuts and 1 whole orange run thru the food chopper. Simmer slowly and pour into jars and seal while hot.—Mrs. Ama Bamer, Wisconsin.

Sweet Pickled Crab Apples, Peaches or Pears

2 lb. brown sugar or
3 lb. white sugar
1 pt. vinegar

1 pt. water
1 oz. stick cinnamon
few cloves

½ peck peaches or apples

Bring the sugar, cinnamon and water and vinegar to boil. Then put in the peeled peaches or apples, and boil till tender. —Mrs. Nick Huebschen, Wisconsin.

Cherry Jam

1 qt. pitted cherries
½ c. water

8 c. sugar
juice of 1 lemon

1 c. commercial pectin

Measure the cherries which have been slightly crushed into a kettle and add water and lemon juice. Stir until mixture begins to boil, then cover kettle and let simmer 10 min. Add sugar and mix well. Use hot fire and stir constantly. Boil hard for 1 min. Remove from stove, stir in pectin, and skim and let stand, with occasional stirring, for 5 min., no longer. Pour into sterilized glasses and paraffin at once.—Clara Morris, Ia.

Carrot Honey

6 c. cooked carrots, put
through sieve
6 c. granulated sugar

1 lemon
2 oranges

Cook until thick, like honey.—Mrs. Bertha Swick, Michigan.

Spiced Apple Jelly

3 c. apple juice
3 ¼ c. sugar
½ c. cider vinegar
½ tsp. cinnamon
½ tsp. nutmeg

Cook until it jells and pour in glasses.—Mrs. B. L. Benson, Minnesota.

Apricot and Pineapple Jelly

For 4 qt. of fresh ripe apricots, use 1 qt. pineapple. Make a syrup as you would for peaches and cook the apricots, which have been sliced. Until tender enough to pierce with a fork. Add the pineapple and cook until it is heated thru. Seal in fruit jar.—Mrs. C. H. Fenner, Texas.

Cranberry Jelly

1 qt. cranberries
2 c. boiling water
2 c. sugar

Pick over and wash berries. Put in pan with boiling water, and boil gently for 20 min. Rub through a sieve and boil 2 min. Add sugar and boil 3 min. Turn into molds or glasses. Commercial pectin may be used if jelly will not jell.—Mrs. W. L. West, Colorado.

Watermelon-Rind Preserves

Wash peeled watermelon rind and let stand over night with an equal quantity of sugar over it. (Yes, I soak it in salted water first, sometimes, but I don't think the preserves made in that way quite so delicious. For one thing, unless the rind is rinsed and soaked in clear water many times it will taste of the salt). In the morning put the pieces of rind, which were cut in very small pieces, over a slow fire to cook in the juice drawn out by the sugar. Boil until transparent; then add a small can of crushed pineapple to complete the best preserves you ever ate. Should you have more juice after cooking than desirable save the syrup left over for more preserves, using less sugar next time, or put it away for mincemeat. A little of these preserves adds to the flavor of a fruitcake.—Kathryn G. Woodside, New Mexico.

Jelly

3 c. juice
6 ½ c. sugar
1 c. liquid pectin

Use about 3 ½ lb. ripe fruit and do not peel but remove pits and crush thoroughly. Add ½ c. water. Stir till it boils, cover and simmer 5 min. Place fruit in jelly bag and extract all the juice. Measure sugar and juice into large pan, stirring and bring to a boil. At once, add the liquid pectin and keep stirring. Boil for ½ min. Remove from fire and let stand 1 min. and skim and seal hot.—Mrs. W. O. Linch, Texas.

Ripe Tomato Preserves

Put thru the food chopper the following:

Ripe tomatoes, apples and 1 orange. For every 2 c. of ground tomatoes and 2 c. apple; add 3 c. sugar. Boil all together till smooth.—Mrs. Louis Loveness, Minnesota.

Ginger Pear

8 lb. pears, wind falls may be used	4 oranges
8 lb. sugar, granulated	4 lemons

½ lb. preserved ginger or crystalized ginger may be used. Pears should be hard. Put pears, orange and lemon peel and ginger through grinder. Combine with other ingredients and cook slowly until thick or until mixture becomes a pretty amber color. Seal hot. Excellent served with fowl or pork.—Mrs. Perry M. Stevens, Illinois.

Citron
(like that you buy in store)

Cut citron into about eights, remove seeds, and let stand about 6 hr. in salt water, drain, rinse and boil in water till nearly clear. Drain and carefully put into heavy syrup made of sugar and water about half and half, cook until clear. Lift with a skimmer onto plates and stand in the sun about 2 or 3 hrs. to harden. Pack in glass jars. It keeps indefinitely.— Miss Leona Peterson, Nebraska.

Cherry or Strawberry Sun Preserves

Clean your fruit as you would for canning, to each pound of fruit, allow 1 lb. sugar. Put sugar on the fruit, and place on the stove, boil for 25 min. Pour into shallow vessels, dripping pans, or some other thing (nothing of tin or aluminum) and cover with glass. Place somewhere in the strong sunlight. When they become quite sirupy they are ready to seal in jars and put away.—Miss Ethel Funkhouser, Kansas.

Delicious Strawberry Preserves

2 c. berries	3 c. sugar
	½ of a lemon

Put all on slow fire till sugar melts, then put on brisk fire and boil for 10 min., skimming all the time. Pour out in a pan, let stand till next day, lifting them over several times thru the day so the juice mixes well with the berries. Can cold and seal or put on parafin. The use of the lemon puffs up the berries to about twice their ordinary size.—Mrs. Joe Rarick, Kansas.

CANDY

Patience Candy

Take quite a large pan, a kettle is best, so it won't boil over. Put 1 c. of granulated sugar in, put over the fire and stir until it is melted, it gets brown like syrup, after all is melted put in 1 scant c. of sweet milk in which has been dissolved a pinch of soda, about the size of a bean, do not get scared now and think you have spoiled it but stir and let boil smooth, then add a second c. of sweet milk scant and 2 c. sugar, butter the size of an egg. Boil until it forms a soft ball when dropped in cold water. Remove from fire and beat until it starts to grain. Walnuts are very good in it. The brown sugar gives it enough flavor and color. If you wish this candy may be rolled like Wurst, spread powdered sugar on a table. When it is cool enough and starts to grain put on the powdered sugar and start to roll don't fold it but just push ends together and keep on rolling till cold then it will stay nicely.—Magdalena Jax, Minn.

Peanut Brittle

1 tbsp. butter	4 c. white sugar
1 tsp. salt	1½ c. syrup
1 pt. water	

Add ½ lb. peanuts or cocoanut when it starts to boil. Cook until good and brown and thick and then add 1 tsp. soda, stirring well. Pour on buttered plates.—Mrs. H. G. Boughten, N. D.

Divinity Candy

3 c. granulated sugar	1 c. nut meats
½ c. white Karo syrup	2 egg whites
⅔ c. water	1 pinch salt

Boil sugar and syrup and water together till it will form a soft ball in water. Then pour ½ slowly over beaten egg whites and put remainder back on fire and boil till it will form a hard ball in water then pour all together and beat till it commences to get stiff then add nut meats and 1 tsp. of vanila. Pour on buttered platter and cool and cut in squares.—Mrs. Chas. H. Musch, Ia.

Date Loaf

1 lb. dates	2 c. sugar
½ lb. nut meats	1 c. milk
Heaping tsp. butter	Flavoring

Cook milk, sugar and butter to soft ball, take from fire, stir in chopped nut meats and chopped dates. Beat until too heavy to move spoon. Turn out on clean cheese cloth. Sprinkle with a mixture of powdered sugar and corn starch. Roll firmly like sausage. Put in ice box over night or any cold place. Cut in thin slices with sharp knife and dust with powdered sugar. Very pretty mixed with divinity fudge.—Mrs Fred J. Stolp, S. Dak.

Fruit Roll

1½ c. sugar
1 c. cream
1 tsp. butter
1 tsp. vanilla
1 c. each fig, seedless
    raisins, and dates
½ c. each English walnuts and pecans

Bring sugar, cream and butter to soft ball. Beat and then add ground fruit and nuts. Stir as long as possible then knead with hands until well mixed. Then roll out like a jelly roll. Wrap in a dampened cloth and waxed paper and put away in a cool place to ripen for 2 or 3 weeks.—Mrs. Harley G. Lofton, Nebr.

Carmels

2 c. granulated sugar
2 c. cream
1¾ c. syrup
1 c. butter
1 c. nuts

Boil all together except the nuts and ½ of cream. Boil 30 min. Then add the last c. of cream and boil until it makes a hard ball. Add nuts and pour into a buttered pan.—Mrs. T. P. Patterson, Kansas.

Mexican Caramels

Melt 1 c. sugar in frying pan, over a slow fire. When dissolved, add 1 c. water or milk. Melt again, add 1 c. white or brown sugar. Cook to soft ball stage. Add 1 tbsp. butter and ½ c. nut meats. Beat until creamy and pour on buttered plates, when set mark in squares.—Mrs. Wm. J. Barlow, Wis.

Penoche

4 c. light brown sugar
2 c. cream
1 c. nuts
2 tbsp. butter

Boil the ingredients together to the soft ball stage. When cooked remove from fire and cool before beating. When cool add nuts and 1 tsp. vanilla.—Miss Faye Mikles, Ia.

Cracker Jack

½ c. New Orleans or any good brand cooking molasses
1 c. granulated sugar
1 tbsp. butter
1 tbsp. vinegar
¼ tsp. soda

Stir well before putting on stove, but do not stir while boiling sugar and molasses, vinegar and butter together, but when cooked so it will thread or form a firm soft ball in water, add soda and stir well before stirring it well through corn which should be in a large pan or buttered bowl (if in a wooden bowl you can chop fine if you like) also add peanuts after which spread about ¾ inch thick in a dripping pan. Pound or press with a board till cool. When it can be cut in squares with a sharp knife. If molasses flavor is wanted more pronounced use 1 c. molasses and ½ c. sugar.—Mrs. John Craig, Mich.

Creamy Fudge

2 tbsp. butter
3 c. sugar
¼ c. corn syrup (white)

1 c. undiluted evap. milk
¼ tsp. salt
¾ c. nut meats

Put the butter into a sauce pan and let it melt and brown over slow fire not too brown. Then add other ingredients with exception of the nuts. Boil until a soft ball forms when a little is tried in cold water. Cool until lukewarm; add the nuts and beat until creamy. Pour on buttered plates and cut in squares. For chocolate fudge add 3 squares chocolate before cooking.—Miss Agnes Tellman, Mo.

Fudge

2 c. sugar
1 c. milk
1 tsp. butter

1½ squares chocolate
1 pinch salt
1 tsp. vanilla

Place sugar, milk and chocolate in a saucepan and boil 10 min. or until it makes a soft ball in cold water. Take from fire, do not stir, add butter and let cool. When cool add vanilla and beat until creamy. Pour in buttered pan and cut in squares.— Dorothy Goss, Mont.

Honey Fudge

½ c. milk (condensed)
1 pinch salt
1 pinch soda
¼ c. honey

1 c. cane sugar
1 c. brown sugar
2 tbsp. butter
2 tbsp. cocoa

Mix sugar, condensed milk and salt together. Cook slowly for 5 min. Add honey and pinch soda. Cook until firm ball stage. Remove from heat, add butter and beat vigorously until soft enough to form flat cakes when dropped from a spoon. Pour into buttered plates and when cool cut into squares.—Mrs. Oscar W. Krueger, Ia.

Mexican Orange Candy

1 c. granulated sugar
1½ c. rich sweet milk
2 c. sugar, granulated

1 c. nut meats
Grated rind of 2 oranges
Pinch salt

½ c. butter

Melt the first cup of sugar in a large kettle, while the milk is scalding in double boiler. When the sugar is melted to a rich yellow, add hot milk all at once stirring it well. It will boil up quickly so be sure to use a good sized kette. Add the 2 c. sugar to this mixture, stirring until dissolved and cook until it forms almost a hard ball in water (238°). Just before it is done add the grated orange rind, the salt, butter and nut meats. Beat until creamy and pour into a buttered platter to cool. This candy is as delicious as it is unusual.—Mrs. S. W. Douglass, Kansas.

WRITE YOUR RECIPES HERE

CANNING

Okra

Use young and tender pods. Wash them
Blanch them for 3 min.
Pack while hot

Fill with hot salt brine:
1 tbsp. salt
1 qt. water
Fill to inch of top

Process 1½ hr. or pressure cook 30 min. at 10 lbs. pressure. Cool and store.—Rosa Lee Mazy, Tex.

Canning Tomatoes

Select solid, ripe tomatoes, skin and cut in suitable pieces. Pack into sterilized jars, quarts and when half full sprinkle with ½ tsp. salt. Finish filling the jar then add another ½ tsp. salt. Put on covers and screw lightly.

Cook in steam cooker 20 or 25 min. and in pressure 15 or 20. Screw caps on tight as soon as they are removed from the cooker.—Frieda Kempf, N. Dak.

Canning Pimentoes

Take pimentoes of equal size and remove the stem ends, seeds and inner white fibers. Cut in halves and pour boiling water over them. Let stand 3 min. Repeat until they have been in the iced water 3 times. Drain for the last time and place in glass jars. Take equal parts of good vinegar and water and to a pt. of each add a c. sugar and bring to a boil. Let cool. When perfectly cool, pour over the peppers and seal. If poured over hot it will wilt the peppers and fade them. Sweet green peppers can be prepared the same way.—Mrs. C. M. Le-Van, Mo.

Canned Beets

Boil beets until tender, peel and slice if you wish. To 1 qt. of vinegar add 1 c. sugar and 1 tsp. salt, let come to a boil, add beets and boil 5 min. then can. Beets canned this way will keep for years.—Mrs. Jess Webster, Mo.

Drying Corn

Select nice tender corn just right for the table. Shuck and silk. Have a large kettle of boiling water ready to drop corn in. Cook from 5 to 10 min. or until the milk is set. Slice from the cob with a thin bladed knife, going over the cob twice, not cutting too deep the first time. Place on a clean sheet or cloth and put in sun to dry. If there is a good breeze and lots of sun this will dry in 1½ days the longest time. Heat a little in over before putting away. Cool and seal in boxes. When ready to use soak over night and cook as fresh corn.—Mrs. W. R. Maxwell, Mo.

Corn

Cut corn off the cob and fill qt. jars with it. To every qt. add 1 scant tbsp. salt and fill jars with water. Seal the jars air tight, put jars into canner, cover with water about 3 or 4 inches over tops and boil for 3 hrs. Be sure to time the cooking after the water starts to boil. Be sure the lids are perfectly tight when you remove them from the hot water. 7 doz. ears sweet corn make 9 qts. canned corn.—Mrs. W. B. Leon, Okla.

Canned Pimentoes

Select sound, uniform peppers of med. size. Remove all seeds and veins, through the stem end. To peel, place the peppers in a hot oven, from 6 to 10 min. (until the skin blisters and cracks) being careful to keep from burning. Remove the skins with a slender paring knife. Flatten the pepper and pack in horizontal layers. The peppers should be tightly packed to fill jar but do not mash. No water is used. The processing brings out of the peppers a thick liquor, which almost covers them in a can or jar, and if mixed with water, makes an unpleasant, shiny mixture. The jars should be well filled. Cap the cans, and process pt. jars for 20 min., qt. jars for 30 min. The processing is the ordinary cold pack method.—Miss Elizabeth Bennett, Ark.

Apple Butter

With cider:	Without cider:
30 gal. raw cider	16 gal. water
20 gal. cored apples	20 gal. apples
30 lbs. sugar	2 qts. vinegar
	30 lbs. sugar

Either of these recipes will make about 15 gallons of butter.—Mrs. Harry Netsey, Ohio.

Cherries for Garnishing

Wash and stone 6 lbs. cherries. Place in stone jar and cover with vinegar. Allow to stand 48 hours. Drain off vinegar. Weigh fruit, and to every lb. fruit add 1 lb. sugar. Place in stone jar alternately layers of cherries and sugar. Cover and let stand, stirring up twice daily from bottom of jar, four days. Pack in jars, and cover with sugar syrup formed in stone jar. Seal.—Miss Beaulah Rumble, Ill.

Grape Juice

Put a cupful of ripe, stemmed grapes and ½ cup sugar into a quart jar; fill with briskly boiling water; seal and store in a cool place. When wanted in the winter, the juice will be found clear and delicious.—Mrs. R. A. Fansher, Okla.

Pumpkin

Wash and pare a pumpkin. Cut in pieces about 2 inches square. Put on stove and cook until it is a butter. To 1 qt. of butter add:

1 tsp. salt	1 tsp. cinnamon
1 tsp. mace	¼ tsp. allspice
1 tsp. nutmeg	2 c. sugar

Boil about 10 min. and seal in glass jars while boiling hot. To make a pie, open pumpkin and to one cup of the pumpkin add:

1 egg	½ c. cream
½ c. milk	½ c. sorghum

Line a pastry pan with a rich crust. Pour in mixture and bake in a very slow oven. Serve with whipped cream that is flavored with vanilla and sweetened to taste.—Mrs. C. D. McLain, Mo.

Canned Vegetables for Soup in Winter

The following recipe is a great time saver to the busy housewife. All the ingredients for good vegetable soup are found in a small can, thus preventing many extra trips to the cellar. Also it is of benefit to the housewife who does not have access to the fresh vegetable markets in winter.

½ bu. tomatoes	2 bunches carrots
2 heads cabbage	(about 10)
12 large onions	12 stalks celery
18 ears corn	4 green peppers

Parsley and salt (season to taste)

Blanch, peel and quarter tomatoes. Put all the other vegetables through the food grinder. Add these to tomatoes, put in a large kettle or pan and cook for 1 hr., stirring frequently to prevent scorching. When done the mixture is rather thick. Seal immediately in glass jars which have been kept hot in boiling water. For the average family, it is better to use pint jars. Open and use with meat stock. If desired, diced potatoes may be added to meat stock about 15 min. before vegetables. Cook until vegetables have had time to heat through and soup is ready to serve. This recipe makes from 22 to 24 pints.—Mrs. Ella Bunton, Ohio.

Tomatoes Canned for Slicing

Sterilize jars and lids. Ripe, firm tomatoes. Rub over tomatoes with back of knife to loosen skin. Peel, place in cans, add 1 tsp. salt to each qt. Pour hot water until all space is filled. Seal tight and place in pan, canner, boiler or any vessel of hot water or so the jars can be put in without breaking. Let stand until cold. They keep perfectly. If not cooked too much in hot water they will readily slice. I have used ½ gal. and 1 gal. syrup pails and put the lid on just as I get them, no extra seal, they keep fine. Be sure cans are bright and clean.—Bertha M. Phelps, Nebr.

Meat Cure

We have used this recipe to cure meat butchered in mid-summer for harvest without losing one pound of meat, using a cold water tank to remove the animal heat and the meat comes out looking as clean and cooks to a rich red color.

Cool meat, cut and place in barrel. Cover with cure, and weigh. For each 1 cwt. meat:

12 lbs. salt	4 oz. salt petre
5 lbs. cane sugar	4 oz. soda

Dissolve soda and salt petre in water separately. Boil salt, sugar and salt petre and skim and let cool, add soda and pour over meat. Leave the brine on 6 or 7 days, and if you wish to smoke it soak in cold water 3 or 4 hrs., wash and hang to dry a few days then smoke.—Mrs. Walter J. Jones, Nebr.

Mince Meat Canning

4 lbs. cooked beef ground	4 c. sweet cider
1 lb. suet ground	5 c. brown sugar
6 apples chopped	4 c. Karo syrup
½ lb. citron	3 nutmegs grated
2 lbs. currants	2 tsp. of each salt, mace,
2 lbs. raisins	cloves, cinnamon
2 c. vinegar	

Bring to slow boil until suet and apples are cooked. Add juice of one lemon and a little pepper. If needed add a little water while cooking. Put into fruit jars and seal while hot.—Alice Arndt, S. Dak.

Preparation for Canning Chicken

Kill at least six hrs. before drawing. Remove feathers, bleed well and cool thoroly. Singe, wash with soap and water or dry soda or bran.

DRAWING—Remove feet, wings and thighs. Sever drumsticks from thighs at joints. From wing joint cut open skin on neck. Insert fingers into the opening and pull out crop without severing it completely from the body. Half way down back insert knife, close to backbone. Find the cut under shoulder blades, break and remove them at joints. Find cartilage on ribs, begin at wing joint and cut through cartilages. Extend cut through cartilages on ribs to and around pelvic bone. Insert hand into body cavity and carefully loosen intestines, lungs, etc. from body. Cut around them, entirely freeing them from body. Hold carcass firmly with one hand, and with the other gently pull out all intestines, drawing toward the head.

CANNED CHICKEN—Place in drumstick. Next place in thigh. Place two wings next to thigh, fitting elbow of one wing into the other. Place neck in center of jar, with rib end down. This acts as a support for remaining pieces and allows heat to quickly penetrate center of jar. Cover neck with back. Spread white meat on top of back. Fit in remaining pieces. Completely fill jar. Add 2 level tsp. salt to each qt. jar. Place on jar ring, partly seal jar. Sterilize. Process in hot water for 3½ hrs. or in steam pressure cooker for 1 hr. at 15 lbs. Remove from canner and can immediately. Meat juices, in canned meats, should form into jelly.—Mrs. Katie Franklin, Maryland.

To Corn Beef

1 c. salt
½ c. brown sugar
Lump of salt petre size hazelnut
3 qts. water

Boil together until salt is dissolved; let cool and pour over meat. Ready to use in about six days—Mrs. M. Rose, Mo.

Chili Con Carne

6 lbs. beef, ground not too fine
2 lbs. chili beans (soaked over night)
½ tsp. chili powder
1 gal. cold water
Salt to taste

Cook slowly for 5 hrs. Fill into jars and cook 2½ hrs. in water bath. These keep fine and taste so good in the summer time when one has so much to do.—Mrs. M. C. Ott, Kan.

Tenderloins

1 gal. water
1 heaping c. sugar
¾ c. salt
1 tbsp. salt petre

Mix ingredients and bring to boil. Place tenderloin which has been cut into pieces about six inches long, into the solution and boil 40 min. Pack meat in a stone jar and cover with solution and when cold finish covering top with lard. This will keep indefinitely.—Mrs. Fern Stacy, Kan.

Kraut

Cut cabbage fine and put in fruit jars. Push it in tight. Put 1 level tbsp. salt to each ½ gal. Pour boiling water in can till full. Seal air tight so they won't spoil. Cans may spoil after they have been put away but do not bother them and they will be all right.

PICKLES

Corn Salad

18 ears corn
2 green peppers
1 head cabbage
3 onions
5 c. sugar
¼ c. salt
¼ c. prepared mustard
5 c. vinegar
Chop fine, boil and seal while hot.—Mrs. C. F. Crocket, Ariz.

Chili Sauce

30 ripe tomatoes
3 large onions
2 red peppers
3 green peppers
4½ c. vinegar
2½ c. brown sugar
3 tbsp. salt

2 tsp. each of ground cinnamon, nutmeg, cloves, allspice, ginger and mustard tied in white cloth. Scald and peel tomatoes, chop or mash to a pulp with onions and peppers, put in enameled pan with the vinegar, sugar, salt and spices. Bring to boil stirring frequently to prevent sticking, boil sauce until it begins to thicken, usually 1 hr. is required. Put into bottles or jars and seal hot. This is fine in cold weather with soup, beans or meat.—Mrs. B. F. Wolfert, N. Dak.

Sweet Pickles
(Wonderfully Delicious Pickles)

Wash cucumbers, make brine that will hold up an egg. Soak cucumbers in brine for 3 days. Take out of brine and soak in clear water for 3 days. Take out of water and split the cucumbers, put in weakened vinegar to taste and add 1 tbsp. powdered alum to a dishpan of pickles. Simmer for 2 hr. Do not boil but so hot you can hardly stir them by hand. Drain again. To 1 pt. vinegar add 2 qt. sugar, let come to a boil and add: 1 oz. each of stick cinnamon, cloves (whole), allspice, and pour over the pickles. Pour off for 3 mornings heat and add 1 c. vinegar, 2 c. sugar each morning. On the third morning they are ready to pack and seal. They must be split for they will shrivel if left whole.—Mrs. Roy Derickson, Ia.

Sweet Pickles, Watermelon

4 c. sugar
1 tbsp. whole cloves
2 tbsp. cinnamon
2 c. vinegar
Watermelon rind

Pare the rind and cut in 2 in. squares then cook tender in boiling water. Just water enough to cover. Put the vinegar, sugar in a kettle then add the spices (tied in a cloth bag). Boil mixture just 10 min. then cook slowly about 1 hr. or till syrup is thick. Add the rind and simmer 1 hr. Can.—Mrs. Andrew Mier, Ia.

Green Tomato Pickles

½ peck green sliced tomatoes
1 c. salt
1 qt. vinegar

2 c. brown sugar
1 tbsp. each allspice, cinnamon
1 tsp. nutmeg

Cover the tomatoes with the salt and let stand over night and drain well in the morning. Add the above mixture and boil together until tender and put in sterilized jars and seal.— Odessa Finley, Ia.

Mustard Pickles

1 qt. chopped green tomatoes
1 qt. chopped cabbage
1 qt. chopped onions

1 qt. green beans
1 can kidney beans
1 can lima beans
1 qt. chopped cucumbers

Hot and sweet peppers (both green and ripe) to taste. Salt and drain over night, the green tomatoes, cabbage and onions. Cook the green beans until tender but not soft. Then add the rest of the ingredients and mix well. Dressing:

2 qts. vinegar
1 qt. water
3 c. sugar

2 c. flour
1 tbsp. whole mixed spices
2 tbsp. ground mustard

Enough tumeric to color

Cook until thick. Add vegetables and simmer 30 min.— Pauline Frazier, Mo.

Olive Oil Pickles

Slice as for serving, 50 medium sized cucumbers. Dressing:

1½ c. olive oil
½ c. mustard seed (white)

½ c. mustard seed (black)
1 tbsp. celery seed

1 qt. vinegar

Salt cucumbers and let stand over night in the water brine. In the morning cover with dressing and seal in pint jars. No cooking required.—Mrs. Herman Palmer, Minn.

Saccharine Pickles

1 gal. vinegar
1 c. salt
½ c. mustard

½ c. ground horseradish
1 c. sugar
1 handful mixed spices

1 tsp. saccharine

Mix all together well and pour over pickles, which have been washed and had boiling water poured over them. Let stand all night and in the morning wipe and pack in sterilized jars and seal after pouring the above solution over them.—Mrs. Ira Pearsale, Wis.

Plum Catsup

5 lb. plums, wild
2 c. brown sugar
1 pt. vinegar
1 tbsp. salt
1 tbsp. pepper
1 tbsp. cinnamon
½ tbsp. cloves

Cover plums with water and boil until very tender. Run thru colander and add other ingredients. Cook 20 min. and seal.— Wilma B. Thomas, S. Dak.

Catsup

Boil ripe tomatoes in own juice till real soft. Strain thru flour sieve. To 1 qt. strained juice add:

½ c. sugar
½ c. vinegar
1 tsp. salt
½ tsp. ginger
½ tsp. nutmeg

Cook till thick and seal in bottles when cold.—Mrs. Fred Kaupp. S. Dak.

Bordeaux Sauce

2 qt. chopped green
   tomatoes
4 qt. chopped cabbage
6 large onions chopped
5 red peppers chopped
2 lb. sugar
2 oz. celery seed
2 oz. mustard seed
1 tsp. tumeric
4 tbsp. salt
2 qt. vinegar

Mix and cook slowly for 1 hr. Seal in fruit jars.—Mrs. C. C. Stocker, Mo.

WAFFLES, PANCAKES, ETC.

Waffles

2 c. flour
4 tsp. baking powder
½ tsp. salt
2 eggs, beaten light
1½ c. sweet milk
4 tbsp. melted butter

Sift dry ingredients, cut shortening into flour. Separate eggs, beat eggs, add to milk, beat into flour mixture, lastly add egg white well beaten. Make 6 waffles.—Mrs. T. V. Hays, Texas.

Dutch Honey
(Delicious with waffles or pancakes)

1 c. sugar
1 c. white syrup
1 c. sweet cream

Boil to the consistency of syrup. Flavor to taste or leave plain. Serve cold.—Ida Thompson, Oklahoma.

Graham Cakes

1 egg
½ c. sugar
Pinch of salt
2 tbsp. melted butter
1 tsp. soda
1½ c. sour milk
½ c. flour
1 c. graham

Mix dry ingredients, add melted butter and beaten egg to sour milk; pour into dry ingredients. Beat thoroughly. Pour in well greased muffin cups and bake in quick oven (400 degrees).—Rush E. Hanna, Kansas.

Buckwheat Griddle Cakes

Soak ½ cake of yeast at night and mix 1 c. graham flour and 2 c. of buckwheat, 1 tsp. salt, and moisten with warm water to make thick batter. Add 2 tbsp. molasses. Cover and let rise until morning. In morning, stir batter down and thin with little warm water and 2 tbsp. sugar. If any sour odor, add ¼ tsp. soda dissolved in warm water, and bake on griddle.—Mrs. Wm. E. Parker, Nebraska.

Rice Griddle Cakes

1 c. boiled rice
1 c. milk
1 tbsp. shortening
1 tsp. salt
1 egg
1 c. flour
2 tsp. baking powder

Mix rice, milk, melted shortening, salt and well beaten egg. Stir in flour and baking powder, which has been sifted together. Mix well, bake on hot greased griddle and serve immediately.—Mrs. J. W. Haggard, Missouri.

Crumb Griddle Cakes

1½ c. stale bread crumbs	½ c. flour
1½ c. sweet milk	½ tsp. salt
3 eggs well beaten	4 tsp. baking powder
	1 tsp. fat

Soak crumbs in milk, add beaten eggs, then flour, sifted with other dry ingredients. Add melted fat. Beat good, drop on hot griddle. Cook on one side until edge is brown and cake is bubbly, then turn and cook on other side.—Mrs. Holvor Jameson, Minnesota.

Buckwheat Cakes Without Yeast

2 c. buckwheat flour	1 tbsp. molasses
1 c. white flour	2 tsp. baking powder
1 egg	1 tsp. salt

Add enough sweet milk to make a batter.—Mrs. Paul Huntley, Colorado.

Doughnuts (Polish)

Cunchies

1 cake compressed yeast (dissolved in lukewarm water)
1 pt. sweet milk (just warm)
Flour enough to make stiff batter

Let rise until light	1 c. sugar
4 eggs well beaten	¾ c. butter

Cream together sugar and butter. Add eggs and butter and flour enough to make a stiff batter as thick as you can mix with a spoon; let rise again, roll out and cut with small biscuit cutter. Let stand to rise and be sure to keep warm. Fry in hot grease, like doughnuts. Then roll in powdered sugar. These are delicious.—Mrs. J. W. Brogan, Iowa.

Pond Lillies

Break an egg into a small mixing bowl; a large cup will do, add a pinch of salt and all the flour you can mix into the egg. Take a small portion of the dough at a time, keeping the remainder covered up, roll out as thin as possible, then cut into round cakes. Cut edges of each cake 8 times, but do not cut thru the center. Dampen the center of 1 cake with a drop of water and lay another cake on it. Then place in very hot fat, keeping the center down with a clothespin. The cut edges will curl up around the clothespin, making them look like pond lillies. These can be filled with any kind of filling, such as creamed peas, creamed chicken, whipped cream or anything desired.—Mrs. G. Lewis, Montana.

Prize Doughnuts

2 eggs	2 tsp. cream tartar
1 c. sugar	1 tsp. soda
1 c. sweet milk	⅓ tsp. grated nutmeg
1 tbsp. melted butter	Pinch of salt

Flour to make soft dough

Beat the eggs and add sugar. Dissolve soda in milk and add melted butter. Sift cream of tartar with some of the flour; add nutmeg. Roll out and fry in hot deep lard.—Mrs. T. A. Sinz, Wisconsin.

Old Fashioned New England Doughnuts

1 c. mashed potatoes	½ c. sweet milk
2 tbsp. butter	4 tsp. baking powder
2 eggs	Nutmeg or flavoring
1 c. sugar	Vanilla
½ tsp. salt	Flour

Beat eggs till thick, add potatoes, butter, sugar. Sift dry ingredients with flour. Alternately add milk and flour to first mixture. Roll out about ½ in. thick, cut and fry in hot fat.— Mrs. Oscar Haugen, Wisconsin.

Cracker Dumplings

½ lb. oyster crackers	Boiling water
Butter size of hazel nut	1 egg

Pinch of salt

Crisp crackers in oven, then roll fine nd add salt, butter and water to moisten them thoroughly. When cool, add egg, well beaten. Form into balls, drop into meat stew, boiling. Let boil for 10 min. These are novel and delicious and easy to make. They are fine with brown gravy, if boiled in water and the gravy poured over.—Mrs. Mae Lucas, Nebraska.

Tomato Dumplings

1 qt. tomatoes	2 c. flour
2 slices bacon	½ c. milk
Salt and pepper	¼ tsp. salt
1 egg	2 tsp. baking powder

Cut the bacon in small pieces and fry, add tomatoes, salt and pepper to taste. Let come to boil, beat egg, add milk, sift baking powder and salt with the flour. Mix and drop by tsp. into the tomatoes. Keep boiling but do not cover, turn when light.—Mrs. Anna Meek, Michigan.

Egg Noodles

Sift a pint of flour into your mixing bowl and make a well in the middle as you would if making soda biscuits. Beat two eggs well and add to them ½ tsp. salt. Drop into the well in the flour mix flour in until it is as stiff as you can mix it.

Flour your bread board and remove noodle dough to the board; roll into very thin sheet, adding flour as needed to prevent sticking. Allow to dry for 1 hr. if possible. If you have not time for drying they must be floured very thickly before rolling. Roll the sheet into a cylinder and cut across. To cook, drop into boiling meat broth or chicken soup. Delicious with stewed chicken and good with any stewed fowl or meat. Boil three min. after they begin to boil. A good sized dish of noodles may be made with 1 egg by adding to the egg as much water as may be held in one half of the egg shell.—N. Maud Bever, Nebraska.

Corn Bread

2 c. corn meal
2 c. sour milk
2 tbsp. melted lard
2 c. sugar
1 tsp. salt
2 eggs
1 tsp. soda
1½ tsp. baking powder
1 tbsp. of cold water

Mix all the dry ingredients by sifting them together and add the sour milk and water with the well beaten eggs, beat good, add the melted lard and beat again. Pour into well greased shallow pans and bake about 30 min. Fine. I put the lard into the baking pan with enough extra to grease pan and set in on the stove to melt while I mix other ingredients. Half of the recipe makes enough for 2 or 3 persons.—Mrs. E. Bollman, Nebraska.

Delicious Rolls
(Will rise in 2 hrs.)

¾ cake compressed yeast
2 c. lukewarm water
1 tsp. salt
1 tbsp. shortening
1 tsp. sugar
Flour

Dissolve yeast in ½ c. lukewarm water. Add salt, shortening and remainder of water. Add enough flour to make a stiff batter. Beat thoroughly and add enough flour to make dough. Knead. Let rise, when doubled in bulk, make into small rolls, greasing each roll before placing in pan. Let rise in warm place for 2 hrs. This recipe will make about 15 large rolls when baked. Bake in quick oven (450 degrees).—Mrs. Ike Hartsell, Texas.

Bread That Never Fails

Yeast:
4 potatoes cooked and mashed fine
½ c. sugar
1 tsp. salt
Mix well together and beat well
1 pt. potato water
½ cake dry yeast dissolved in
½ c. warm water
Mix and leave until potatoes come to the top

Bread:

1 pt. warm water Salt to taste
2 tbsp. sugar ½ c. above yeast
1 tbsp. lard

Mix dough stiff at night, and make out into pans in morning and bake, or push down and leave until noon or night, if you want hot rolls. The older the yeast gets, the better bread it makes.—Mrs. Opie L. Reed, Missouri.

Strawberry Fritters

2 c. fresh strawberries 3 eggs
½ c. sugar 1½ c. sweet milk
1 tbsp. butter 1 tsp. baking powder
Flour

Melt the butter and add to the sugar. Beat the eggs well and add with the milk, to the sugar mixture. Mix well and add the baking powder which has been mixed with flour enough to make a smooth batter. Then stir in the 2 c. fresh strawberries and drop the mixture by spoonfuls into hot fat. Drain and serve with syrup of any flavor.—Mrs. Della Morris, Iowa.

Oatmeal Muffins

Turn 1 c. scalded milk over ⅔ c. oatmeal, and let stand 5 min. Melt 2 tbsp butter, 2 tsp salt and 3 tbsp. sugar and add to oatmeal and milk. Sift in 1½ c. flour and 4 tsp. baking powder and lastly one egg well beaten. Place in greased muffin tins and bake in hot oven (400 degrees).—Mrs. Linnie F. Ericson, Nebraska.

Savory Toast

Soak 1 c. of bread crumbs in 1 c. milk and add to 1½ c. grated cheese that has been slightly softened with 1 tbsp. butter, in a sauce pan. Stir till blended and the cheese melted, then add a beaten egg, salt to tast and a dash of cyenne. Stir till the egg is set and serve on slices of toast with parsley or other garnish.—Miss Arlene M. Bailey, Texas.

Bismarks

½ gal. bread sponge Flour to kneed stiff like
2 large tbsp. lard bread
½ c. sugar

Let raise, then work down when raised again pour ouʋ on floured board or table and roll about ½ inch thick, then cut with knife about 4 in. long and 2 in. wide. Let raise again but not very much, then fry in hot lard like doughnuts. When cool frost with powdered sugar or roll in powdered sugar.—Mrs. Wm. Peterson, South Dakota.

Nut Bread

4 c. flour
2 c. sweet milk
½ c. sugar

4 tsp. baking powder
1 egg
1 tsp. salt

1½ c. nuts chopped fine

Sift flour, baking powder, salt, and sugar. Stir in one egg, well beaten, add milk and nuts. Let rise in bread pans ½ hr. Bake in slow oven 50 min. Excellent for sandwiches.—Nova Sanders, Missouri.

Orange Bread

Grind the peel from 3-4 oranges, place in sauce pan with plenty of cold water to cover and cook till tender, drain. Add 1 c. sugar, and ⅓ c. water and cook till water is evaporated. Cool. Mix together 1 egg, 1 c. sweet milk, 3 c. flour, 4 tsp. baking powder. Add orange mixture. Pour in greased bread pan. Let rise 15 min. Bake 45 min. in moderate oven (350 degrees).—Mrs. Tresmon Miller, Kansas.

Baking Powder Cinnamon Rolls

1 c. either sweet or sour cream (soda if sour cream is used)

Sift all together::
3 c. flour
½ c. sugar

½ tsp. salt
3 tsp. baking powder

2½ tsp. baking powder if soda has been used)

Sift into cream. Add enough liquid so that it can be rolled out flat. Pour melted butter over flat dough and sprinkle sugar and cinnamon and either raisins or sliced apples. Roll up, then cut into cinnamon rolls and bake in hot oven. Eat fresh.— Mrs. Nels Bugstedt, Minnesota.

Baking Powder Biscuit

2 c. flour
2 tbsp. shortening

½ tsp. salt
4 tsp. baking powder

⅔ c. milk or water

Sift flour, baking powder, and salt, together twice. Work in the shortening with 2 knives, gradually add the milk and mix well with a knife to a soft dough. You may add more liquid if it is required. Turn on a floured board and roll out and cut. Then put into pans to bake in very warm oven about 15 min. Brush with butter to give a rich brown exterior. It may be omitted.—Mrs. Lester Wion, Iowa.

Kolaches (Bohemian Fruit Biscuit)

1 pt. sweet milk (scalded and cooled)
5 tsp. melted butter
3 tsp. melted lard

⅛ c. sugar
½ cake compressed yeast
1 tsp. salt
Flour to make med. batter

Fruits for filling may be well boiled apricots, peaches or prunes. Mash boiled fruit thoroughly, add enough juice to make a medium soft mixture, but not runny. Add sugar to suit taste. Put compressed yeast in a ¼ c. of cooled scalded milk. When yeast is dissolved, put it into the remaining milk, add the melted butter and lard, sugar, salt and flour to make a medium dough. Let rise 3 times. Then after the 3rd rising cut dough in small biscuit forms and slightly flatten on a greased pan about 1½ in. apart. Brush with melted butter and let rise until light. Then make small cavities on the top of each biscuit very carefully and fill with a tbsp. of mashed boiled fruit. Let rise about 5-10 min. more and bake in a quick oven until nicely brown about 15-20 min. Delicious with coffee.—Mrs. Louis G. Lasack, Iowa.

SANDWICHES

Sandwiches

Make a sandwich of two thin slices of bread with slice of good cream cheese between, slightly butter outside with softened butter and place in hot skillet and let brown on both sides, which melts the cheese and makes a hot toast sandwich.—Mrs. J. S. Hill, Ohio.

Quick Salad or Sandwich Filling

2 c. cottage cheese
1 c. grated pineapple
To make the mayonnaise:
3 eggs well beaten
½ c. sugar
½ c. sour cream

½ c. nuts chopped fine
Moisten with mayonnaise

½ c. vinegar
½ tsp. salt
1 tsp. dry mustard

Cook in double boiler

Here is a really "quick" sandwich filling for the child with a sweet tooth: 2 tbsp. cocoa, 1 tbsp. sugar, a few drops extract. Moisten so it will spread well, with sweet whole milk or thin cream.—Mrs. Maude Bennett, Texas.

Hot Sandwich Filling

3 c. ground cooked beef
½ c. ground cheese
6 ground pickles
½ c. ground pimento

Season with salt and
paprika
Add: 1 egg
½ c. bread crumbs

Mix well with hands and moisten with broth from meat enough to make a patty mixture. It will keep nicely or it may be used immediately. Shape into patties and fry putting between bread and serve hot.—Mrs. Besie Eiler, Ia.

Delicious Sandwich Spread

To one cup of peanut butter, add 1 c. chopped dates and use for a sandwich spread. It is perfectly delicious, appetizing, and healthful.—Alemeda Maxson, Kansas.

Poinsettia Sandwiches

Mix together equal parts salted almonds very finely chopped and mayonnaise dressing. Spread thin slices bread with creamed butter and almond mixture. Cover with another slice of buttered bread, and spread upper side with thin coating of firm tart, red jelly. Shape like a poinsettia petals and arrange on a plate around a mound of coursely chopped salted almonds. Garnish with water cress or laurel leaves and serve with hot chocolate or coffee.—Etta Lea Spratt, Texas.

Denvers

Beat 1 egg lightly, add 1 slice minced cold boiled ham, 1 tbsp. minced onion, pinch salt.   Place in a hot buttered skillet when partly set, turn the mixture and when raised serve at once between 2 slices of buttered bread.—Mrs. D. Bethlake. Minn.

Tomato Sandwiches

Peal ripe tomatoes without scalding, by first scraping them with the back of a knife, then cut into thin slices.   Cut bread into very thin slices, and spread one slice with butter, and the opposite slice with mayonnaise dressing.   Lay tomatoes between the slices, cut in triangles and serve.—Mrs. N. E. Hibbs, Idaho.

ICE-BOX COOKERY

Chocolate Pinwheel Ice Box Cookies

½ c. butter
½ c. sugar
1 unbeaten egg yolk

3 tbsp. milk
1½ c. bread flour
1½ tsp. baking powder

⅛ tsp. salt

Cream the butter, add sugar gradually, egg yolk, then add sifted dry ingredients alternately with the milk. To ½ the dough add 1 square of melted chocolate. Roll the white in a rectangular sheet ¼ inch thick. Then roll dark dough the same size and thickness and place on top of the white. Roll as for jelly roll. Place in an ice box for 24 hours. When cold and firm slice in ¼ inch slices. Bake in moderate oven.—Mrs. Gertrude Hasenjaeger, Mo.

Overnight Salad. Serves 50

Prepare the day before needed for use. Place in a refrigerator over night.
Dressing:

4 eggs
½ tsp. mustard

½ tsp. salt
½ c. sweet milk

Juice of 1 lemon

Place milk in double boiler, when warm add eggs, mustard and salt. Cook until thick. Remove from stove and add lemon juice.
Salad:

1 pt. whipping cream
½ lb. almonds

1 large can pineapple
1 lb. white grapes

1 lb. marshmallows cut fine

Blanch almonds, drain juice from pineapple, cut in cubes, seed the grapes. Cut marshmallows in small pieces with kitchen scissors. Whip the cream, add almonds, grapes, pineapple, marshmallows. Then stir in dressing. Place in ice box 24 hours before using.—Mrs. Samuel Felt, Kans.

Caramel Pudding

Into a double boiler put 1 qt. milk. Let it come to the boiling point. Mix thoroly 1 c. sugar and ½ c. flour. Slowly add the flour and sugar to the milk. Cook until thick and add yolks of 3 well beaten eggs. When it becomes thick take from fire and flavor with vanilla. Pour into a baking dish. Melt 1 c. granulated sugar without water until it melts and slightly burns. Pour this over the pudding. Make a meringue with the whites of the 3 eggs. Add 6 tbsp. sugar to this meringue. Brown in oven. Place in ice box for 24 hours, for this is much better if it stands at least 24 hours.—Mrs. H. Tweedy, Nebr.

Cream Mellow Pudding

4 c. milk
1 c. sugar
4 tbsp. cornstarch

3 eggs
¼ tsp. salt
1 tsp. vanilla

2 c. whipping cream

Heat the milk in a double boiler. Beat the eggs well, to this add the sugar, salt and cornstarch and mix thoroly. Stir into this the scalded milk and put into double boiler again. Cook until thick, stirring well to keep from lumping. When the cornstarch is thoroly cooked put in a cool place until chilled. Whip the 2 c. cream and add to this. Also add the flavoring. Keep in ice box 24 hours before serving. This is as good as ice cream and not half the trouble.—Mrs. S. D. Petrie, Kan.

Chocolate Ice-Box Pudding

Put 2 squares of chocolate in double boiler. Melt and stir until smooth. Heat 2 c. milk to boiling point. To this add 4 tbsp. corn starch. Beat the whites of 4 eggs until stiff and add to this ½ c. sugar. When the milk mixture is thickened pour this over the egg white mixture. Add half of this mixture to the chocolate. Pour some of the white custard and then some of the dark custard into a mould until both mixtures are used. Set in the ice box 24 hours. Serve with whipped cream. —Mrs. M. G. Stanley, Va.

Ice-Box Pudding

8 graham crackers rolled
fine
½ lb. marshmallows cut in
small pieces

1 box dates, chopped
1 c. nuts, chopped
1 small can condensed
milk

Mix all together the day previous to using. Mould into a loaf, set in ice box until ready to serve. Serve with whipped cream. —Mrs. J. T. Franklin, Ill.

Binola

6 egg whites
1 envelop powdered gela-
tine
1 c. walnut meats chopped
fine

1tsp. vanilla
6 tbsp. sugar
¼ lb. candied cherries
3 bananas

Dissolve gelatine in 3 tbsp. cold water. To this add ¾ c. boiling water, place on stove and stir until gelatine is thoroly dissolved. Cool. Add to sugar, vanilla and stiffly beaten whites of eggs. Stir until it begins to jell, then add fruit and nuts, which have been chopped fine. Pour into narrow deep pan to harden, remove from mold and slice as for ice cream. This should stand at least 24 hours in the ice box.—Mrs. Harvey Paulsen, Iowa.

Nesselrode Pudding

1 envelop powdered gelatine
1 c. cold water
1 c. finely grated cocoanut
⅔ c. sugar

½ c. nut meats
¾ c. chopped dates or raisins
Yolks 5 eggs
2 tsp. vanilla

2 c. milk

Bring milk to boiling point. Beat the yolks of the eggs, to this add the sugar. Stir into the milk and cook 2 min. Remove from stove and add gelatine which has been dissolved in the cold water. Then add the cocoanut, dates, nuts and vanilla. Put in the ice box for 24 hours. Serve with whipped cream. A delicious way to use yolks when baking a white cake.—Mrs. Cleve Butler, Mo.

A Recipe for the Day
Mrs. E. L. Monser, Wenona, Ill.

Take a little dash of water cold
And add a little leven of prayer,
And a little bit of morning gold
Dissolved in the morning air

Add to your meal some merriment
And a thought for kith and kin;
And then, as your prime ingredient,
A plenty of work thrown in.

But spice it all with the essence of love,
And a little whiff of play,
Let the good wise Book and a glance above
Complete the well made day.

HOUSEHOLD HINTS

To Clean Mantles

Those who use either gasoline or coal oil lamps with mantles in them will find when the mantles become smoked, instead of throwing them away, take the salt shaker and shake salt over the mantle while still burning. They will clean up good as new. —Mrs. Bert L. Black, Arizona.

To Keep Juice In Pie

1. Put sugar in pies first and fruit on top and juice will not boil out.

2. If 4 or 5 toothpicks are stuck upright in pies, it will help prevent running over.—Mrs. Peter W. Slowey, S. Dakota.

A Stocking Saver

Paste a piece of velveteen cloth in the heel of your shoe and it will save the stocking very much.—Miss Mildred Christenson. N. Dakota.

Putting Curtains on Rods

I find that when putting curtain rods through curtains if I put a thimble over the end of the rod and push it through the curtain, it does not catch and pull the goods, and goes on much quicker.—Mrs. Otto Skoog, Minn.

For Jams and Pickles

I find that in making jam or marmalade to grind fruit first, in food chopper saves time, and heat. Also good to prepare catsup this way.—Mrs. T. P. Rhodes, Mo.

To Soften Cake Icing

If frosting becomes so hard that it breaks and falls off the cake while cutting it, take a clean cloth and wring it out of very hot water and spread over cake, placing a dry towel over this. The steam will soften the frosting so it can be cut without breaking.—Mrs. Hilton Mesenbring, Minn.

Some Stain Removers

To remove grease spots—Ether is always sure and safe to use.

Iron rust may be removed from delicate fabrics by covering spot thickly with cream of tartar, then twisting cloth to keep cream of tartar over spot; put in a sauce pan of cold water, and heat water gradually to boiling point.

To remove ink or iodine stains—Let stand over night in sour milk.

Perspiration stains—Before washing clothes that have been stained by perspiration, soak them in salt water.

Removing Shell from Cooked Egg

Boiled eggs—After an egg has been boiled, the shell can be quickly removed by first dipping the egg in cold water.

For Sewing on Buttons

To keep buttons of the same size together, fasten them on safety pins and the desired size may be seen at a glance.

A Sprinkling Short Cut

Dip the whisk broom into hot water and use as a sprinkler for sprinkling clothes.—Mrs. Jas B. Gleason, Ia.

Short Cut That Saves Time

For my scrap bag I use a flour sack which contains all kinds of pieces left over from sewing. I pin this sack shut with a safety pin which has a sample of each kind of cloth found within it right on the safety pin. One look at samples and you do not have to search all through the sack which saves time and energy.—Mrs. Fred Koch, Colo.

Pocket Stays

Before sewing pockets to kitchen aprons or children's clothes, baste a strip of self material to the back of the garment where the pocket is to be stitched. Place pocket in position so it comes exactly on top of the basted strip and stitch in place. This makes the pocket firm and it is not likely to tear away from the garment.

For Buttonholes

When making buttonholes in material that frays easily, place a small piece of mending tissue between the two thicknesses of the material and press with a hot iron. Then cut the holes.—Mrs. Easton Hanson, Nebr.

To Unravel Flour Sack

When trying to unravel flour sacks, keep the side with double stitch to the left and begin at the end farthest away.—Mabel Chase, N. Dakota.

A Darning Suggestion

Try using a glass egg when darning dark stockings. It is inexpensive and, being white, enables one to see the hole in the stocking.—Mrs. Wm. J. Vandersperren, Jr., Wisconsin.

Lye Soap

5 lbs. melted and strained grease
1 lb. can of lye dissolved in 3 pts of cold water
1½ tbsp. of borax
½ c. of household amonia

When lye and water mixture is cooled, it is added to the fat and other ingredients and then stirred until thick. The resultant soft soap is poured into a paste board or wooden box lined with waxed paper and set away in a warm dry place to harden. This recipe has been tried and tested and passed on to others and pronounced fine by all.—Miss Hattie M. Thomas, Texas.

Six Useful Shortcuts

1. An old toothbrush used to apply shoe polish will save the hands.

2. When in a hurry, to make jello harden, add only a c. of hot water to dissolve it, then add a c. of cold water. The jello will harden more quickly.

3. When placing away an extra kerosene lamp, place a paper sack over the chimney and it will keep clean and ready for instant use.

4. When children skin the toes of their shoes, shellac it, then polish over and no one can tell where the skinned place was.

5. Use safety razor blades for scraping paint from the windows.

6. Lineoleum will wear much better if varnished when new and waked lightly every month after washing.—Mrs. Laura Enloe, Wisconsin.

Preserving a Husband

Be careful in your selection. Do not choose too young, and take only such varieties as have been reared in a good moral atmosphere. When once decided upon and selected, let that part remain forever settled and give your entire attention to preparation for domestic use. Some insist on keeping them in a pickle, while others are constantly getting them into hot water. Even poor varieties may be made sweet, tender and good by garnishing them with patience, well sweetened by smiles and flavored to taste with kisses. Then wrap well in the mantle of charity and keep warm with a steady fire of domestic devotion and serve with peaches and cream. When thus prepared they will keep for years.—Beulah Ready, Wyo.

INDEX

CANDIES

CANNING

CHEESE AND EGG DISHES

COOKIES

DESSERTS, HOT AND COLD

FISH

FROSTING

170

POULTRY AND GAME

SANDWICHES

SALADS AND SALAD DRESSINGS

SOUPS

VEGETABLES

WAFFLES, PANCAKES, ETC.